PLAYS BY RENAISSANCE AND RESTORATION DRAMATISTS

General Editor: Graham Storey

T[illegible]

VOLUMES IN THIS SERIES

PUBLISHED

The selected plays of Thomas Middleton, edited by David L. Frost: *A Mad World, My Masters; A Chaste Maid in Cheapside; Women Beware Women; The Changeling* (with William Rowley)

The selected plays of Philip Massinger, edited by Colin Gibson: *The Duke of Milan; The Roman Actor; A New Way to Pay Old Debts; The City Madam*

FORTHCOMING

The selected plays of John Marston, edited by Robert Cummings: *Antonio and Mellida; Antonio's Revenge; The Malcontent; The Dutch Courtezan; Sophonisba*

The selected plays of Ben Jonson, edited by Johanna Procter: *Sejanus; Epicoene,* or *The Silent Woman; Volpone; The Alchemist; Bartholomew Fair*

The plays of George Etherege, edited by Michael Cordner; *The Man of Mode; She Would if She Could; The Comical Revenge*

The selected plays of John Webster, edited by Inga-Stina Ewbank and Jonathan Dollimore: *The White Devil; The Devil's Law Case; The Duchess of Malfi*

The plays of William Wycherley, edited by Peter Holland: *Love in a Wood; The Gentleman Dancing Master; The Country Wife; The Plain Dealer*

THE PLAYS OF
CYRIL TOURNEUR

The Revenger's Tragedy
The Atheist's Tragedy

EDITED BY
GEORGE PARFITT
Lecturer in English, University of Nottingham

CAMBRIDGE UNIVERSITY PRESS
CAMBRIDGE
LONDON · NEW YORK · MELBOURNE

Published by the Syndics of the Cambridge University Press
The Pitt Building, Trumpington Street, Cambridge CB2 1RP
Bentley House, 200 Euston Road, London NW1 2DB
32 East 57th Street, New York, NY 10022, USA
296 Beaconsfield Parade, Middle Park, Melbourne 3206, Australia

First published 1978

Printed in Great Britain at the
University Press, Cambridge

Library of Congress Cataloguing in Publication Data

Tourneur, Cyril, 1575?–1626
The plays of Cyril Tourneur.

(Plays by Renaissance and Restoration dramatists)
CONTENTS: The revenger's tragedy. – The atheist's tragedy.
I. Parfitt, George, 1939– II. Tourneur, Cyril, 1575?–1626. The atheist's tragedy. 1978. III. Series.
PR3172.R4 1978 822′.3 77-6621
ISBN 0 521 21697 4 hard covers
ISBN 0 521 29235 2 paperback

PREFACE TO THE SERIES

This series provides the best plays (in some cases, the complete plays) of the major English Renaissance and Restoration dramatists, in fully-annotated, modern-spelling texts, soundly edited by scholars in the field. Although the first three volumes are devoted to Renaissance dramatists, future volumes will present the work of such Restoration playwrights as Etherege and Wycherley.

The introductory matter in each volume is factual and historical rather than critical: it includes, where appropriate, a brief biography of the playwright, a list of his works with dates of plays' first performances, the reasons for the volume editor's choice of plays, a short critical bibliography and a note on the texts used. An introductory note to each play then gives the source material, a short stage-history, and details of the individual editions of that play. Facsimiles of the original or early title-pages are given.

Annotation is of three types. Short notes at the foot of the page are designed to gloss the text or enlarge on its literary, historical or social allusions. At the end of the volume, in two separate appendices, editors have added more substantial explanatory notes and have commented on textual variants.

The volumes are intended for anyone interested in English drama in two of its richest periods, but they will prove especially useful to students at all levels who want to enjoy and explore the best work of these dramatists.

Graham Storey

CONTENTS

INTRODUCTION

Life

Of simple necessity, all accounts of the life of Cyril Tourneur have to begin with the statement that, even by the standards of other Jacobean writers, he is an almost completely obscure figure. Very little is known about him and not very much about his literary output. The most thorough account remains that in Allardyce Nicoll's *World Drama*. He is driven to conjecturing that Cyril Tourneur may be the same man as one William Turner – a conjecture symptomatic of the sort of helplessness the biographer is driven to in this case.

We do not know when Tourneur was born (although from later references to him it is probable that the birth happened between 1570 and 1580); we do not know where he was educated or to what level; we know virtually nothing about his background or family beyond the possibility that he may have been related to one Richard Turner, a connection based on the fact that both men were associated with the Cecil family and with Sir Francis Vere.

Most of the surviving material relevant to Tourneur's life, apart from references to his literary activities, dates from 1613. We know that in December of that year he took official letters from London to Brussels, and in August 1614 James Bathurst, writing to William Trumbull, speaks of 'one Cyril Turner, that belongs to General Cecil and was in former times Secretary to Sir Francis Vere'. We also know that he was arrested in 1617 on order of the Privy Council (although, typically, why remains a mystery) and that he was quickly released on the bond of Sir Edward Cecil. Somewhere around this time he seems to have had a job in the Netherlands, since it is known that he had a pension of £60 a year from the States of Holland. Finally, when Sir Edward Cecil sailed to raid Spanish treasure ships at Cadiz in October 1625 he took Tourneur with him as Secretary of the Council of War. The raid failed and Cecil turned back in November. Plagued by disease, the *Royal Anne*, flagship to the fleet, put over one hundred and fifty men ashore at Kinsale in Ireland: one of these was Tourneur and he died there on 28 February 1626.

In so far as these few pieces of material establish anything, they show that Tourneur was connected with the court and the military, mainly in a secretary-cum-courtier capacity. This, together with the absence of critical references to him as an author, suggests – as Ribner says – that his connection with the theatre 'was probably a brief and incidental one'.[1] Here

1 I. Ribner (ed.), *The Atheist's Tragedy* (London: Methuen, 1964), p. xxi.

again Ribner's 'incidental' is tantalising, for nothing is known about what led Tourneur to write for the stage. The best guess one can make is that lack of other employment led him to seek work with the theatre for a short period (or periods). Granted what we know about the sort of work he did for Vere and Cecil, there would be no major social barrier to his writing for the stage when need arose, but who or what provided his entrée remains unknown.

Works

The Transformed Metamorphosis (1600) – poem.[2]

**Laugh and Lie Down* (1605) – pamphlet.

**The Revenger's Tragedy* (1607) – 'As it hath been sundry times Acted, by the King Majesties Servants': there is no more precise evidence of any contemporary performance.

'A Funeral Poem Upon the Death of the most Worthy and True Soldier Sir Francis Vere' (1609)

The Atheist's Tragedy (1611) – 'As in divers places it hath often beene acted': again, no more definite evidence of contemporary staging exists.

The Nobleman (1612) – a lost play probably acted at Court in February 1612 and around Christmas 1613.

*'Character of Robert Earl of Salisbury' (1612) – prose 'portrait'.

*'A Griefe On the Death of Prince Henrie . . . ' (1613) – poem.

An act of *ye Arraignment of London* (? = *The Bellman of London*) (*c.* 1613) – part of a play. The minor dramatist Daborne wrote to Henslowe that he had given an act of this play to Tourneur to write: whether Tourneur did his share and whether the play was finished, let alone produced, we do not know.

*'On the death of a child but one year old' (1899) – poem.

*'Of my Lady Anne Cecill . . . ' (1660) – poem.

Works marked with an asterisk are not certainly Tourneur's: if they are all deleted we are left with a very slender output indeed, and it includes one play and part of another which have not survived. This, of course, makes the problem of the ascription of *The Revenger's Tragedy* even more difficult than it would otherwise be (see below).

2 The dates given in brackets are dates of publication, except for *The Nobleman* and *ye Arraignment of London.*

A select bibliography

Allardyce Nicoll, *Works of Cyril Tourneur* (New York, 1923; new issue 1963) contains the bulk of the material listed above and has a full account of what is known about Tourneur: its notes are, however, sketchy, and the critical comments of little value. (Editions of *The Revenger's Tragedy* and *The Atheist's Tragedy* are discussed in the Introductory Note to each play.)

Early criticism of Tourneur, which assumed his authorship of *The Revenger's Tragedy*, stressed the 'amorality' of the plays, tending to see the author as directly present in the writing and to emphasise the pathological nature of the dramatist thus inferred. This line is summed up by T.S. Eliot,[3] but more recent writing has been inclined to dwell less on the imagined personality of the writer and more on the plays and their context. John Peter has placed Tourneur in the line of traditional 'complaint' literature, while L.G. Salingar and S. Schoenbaum have emphasised other traditional aspects of the background to *The Revenger's Tragedy.*[4] Other writers have provided useful comments on theological context and on the relationship of these two plays to other drama of their period.[5]

More purely critical discussion has concerned itself mainly with *The Revenger's Tragedy*, but has been strongly influenced by the writer's views on attribution and/or the dramatist's moral position. Thus Ribner sees Tourneur as essentially a Christian moralist – he sees all dramatists this way – and Ornstein also reads *The Revenger's Tragedy* in the context of his overall thesis about the moral weighting of Jacobean tragedy. T.B. Tomlinson, on the other hand, is more concerned

3 *Selected Essays 1917–1932* (London: Faber, 1976), p. 189.

4 J. Peter, *Complaint and Satire in Early English Literature* (Oxford University Press, 1956); L.G. Salingar, '*The Revenger's Tragedy* and the morality tradition', *Scrutiny* VI (1938) (reprinted in R.J. Kaufmann, *Elizabethan Drama* (New York: Galaxy, 1961) p. 208f.); S. Schoenbaum, '*The Revenger's Tragedy*: Jacobean dance of death', *M.L.Q.* XV (1954), p. 201f.

5 e.g. M.H. Higgins, 'The influence of Calvinist thought on Tourneur's *Atheist's Tragedy*', *R.E.S.* XIX (1943); R. Ornstein, *The Moral Vision of Jacobean Tragedy* (University of Wisconsin Press, 1965), p. 121f.; S. Schoenbaum, *Middleton's Tragedies* (New York: Gordian Press, 1970), *passim*; H. Jenkins, 'Cyril Tourneur', *R.E.S.* XVIII (1941).

to show that Tourneur is fully in control of his material.[6] These are probably the best of the primarily critical studies: Tomlinson goes a long way towards establishing Tourneur's artistry, but both Ribner and Ornstein seem to me to beg important artistic questions in their anxiety to show the moral orthodoxy of the dramatist.

(For a select bibliography on the authorship problem and on sources see below.)

A note on texts

I have used the earlier form of the first edition (1611) of *The Atheist's Tragedy* as my copy text and have checked this against the texts of Nicoll and Ribner. For *The Revenger's Tragedy* my copy text is the second issue (1608) of the 1607 first edition: this has been checked against the texts of Nicoll, Gibbons, Ross and Foakes. In both plays I have modernised spelling and punctuation but have avoided emendation wherever possible, while recording important variants in the Textual Notes. Where necessary I have added or amplified stage directions and I have followed modern practice in adding scene divisions. On a number of occasions lineation has been adjusted: I have used my own judgement here, although I have consulted the practice of other editors.

The question of authorship

There is no authorship question so far as *The Atheist's Tragedy* is concerned. The first printing of the play attributes it to Tourneur and there has never been any reason to doubt the ascription. The problem arises with the attribution of *The Revenger's Tragedy* to the same man.

The Revenger's Tragedy was first printed anonymously and the first ascription of it to any named dramatist seems not to come until 1656, when Edward Archer attributed the play to Tourneur in a play list attached to his printing of *The Old Law*. In similar play lists of 1661 and 1671 Francis Kirkman followed Archer, and these three lists provide the only external evidence for giving the play to Tourneur. It has often been pointed out

6 I. Ribner, *Jacobean Tragedy* (Methuen, 1962), p. 72f.; Ornstein, *Moral Vision*, p. 121f.; T.B. Tomlinson, *A Study of Elizabethan and Jacobean Tragedy* (Cambridge University Press, 1964), p. 97f.

that neither Archer nor Kirkman can be relied upon: Schoenbaum, for example, points out that Archer attributes *A Trick to Catch the Old One* to Shakespeare, while Kirkman gives *Lust's Dominion* to Marlowe and both foist the tedious *Mucedorus* on Shakespeare.[7] Such errors naturally cast serious doubt on the attributions of *The Revenger's Tragedy*, especially as they come some fifty years or more after the first edition. But the particular errors just mentioned make some sort of sense. Compilers of play lists usually have a commercial motive, and to ascribe plays to Shakespeare and Marlowe is to claim a dignity for them which might well help sales. It is with this in mind that it is difficult to dismiss the *Revenger's Tragedy* attribution out of hand, for it is hard to see any possible motive for giving that play to a writer as obscure as Tourneur unless the compilers of the lists had access to evidence of his authorship which has now disappeared. So the question remains open: Tourneur cannot be ruled out, but neither can the very real possibility that the play is not his – especially since the Rogers and Ley catalogue of 1656 lists it as anonymous.

One other matter of external evidence needs to be touched on. Hillebrand has pointed to a lawsuit brought by Robert Keysar against Thomas Middleton alleging that the latter failed to deliver to him a play called *The Viper's Brood.*[8] Some critics have taken this play to be the same as *The Revenger's Tragedy*, pointing out that *The Viper's Brood* would be an apt subtitle for the latter play. This suggested link has been attacked by Foakes, whose position was, in turn, questioned by Schoenbaum.[9] It must, I think, be accepted that as external evidence of Middleton's authorship this link is very tenuous: at best it might be part of a case that would need to be very strong on other grounds.

The Archer/Kirkman ascription to Tourneur seems to have been accepted without question until the end of the nineteenth century, since when a Tourneur–Middleton battle has raged intermittently and inconclusively. A summary view of the controversy shows a gradual swing in favour of Middleton, culminating in *The Revenger's Tragedy* being treated as

7 Schoenbaum, *Middleton's Tragedies*, p. 157.
8 H.N. Hillebrand, 'Thomas Middleton's *The Viper's Brood*', *M.L.N.*, XLII (1927), p. 35f.
9 R.A. Foakes, 'On the authorship of *The Revenger's Tragedy*', *M.L.R.*, XLVIII (1953), p. 136; Schoenbaum, *Middleton's Tragedies*, p. 166.

Middleton's by both Barker and Schoenbaum in their books on that dramatist.[10] This movement has lost some of its momentum lately: by the time he came to write *Internal Evidence and Elizabethan Dramatic Authorship* (1967), Schoenbaum had come to doubt his own earlier confidence and to regard the play as anonymous. P.B. Murray (see below) has undergone a modified form of the same sea-change.

Defence of Tourneur's authorship has, wisely, not relied mainly on the play lists: most writers accept that this evidence, at best, establishes a weakish *prima facie* case, and have sought to base their defence on other grounds. Sykes merely asserted his belief in Tourneur, while Miss Ellis-Fermor (following to excess Caroline Spurgeon's approach to Shakespeare's imagery) argued on the basis of alleged similarity between the images of *The Atheist's Tragedy* and *The Revenger's Tragedy*. Her methodology is weak and her conclusions, as Foakes has pointed out,[11] are at least partly vitiated by the parallel research of Mincoff who, having examined the images independently, reached a position diametrically opposite to hers. In 1959 Mrs Ewbank (then Ekblad) started from the Ellis-Fermor/Mincoff impasse and set out to show that if one considered 'the function of imagery as part of dramatic structure and technique' one could defend the pro-Tourneur thesis.[12] Her article is interesting but it seems to depend on a presupposition of what she wants to prove: if you believe in Tourneur to start with, it is not too difficult to produce an argument about his developing mind which has an appearance of plausibility. There is a similar weakness in the essay by Harold Jenkins already mentioned: he too postulates common authorship and proceeds to develop a plausible-seeming theory of psychological biography for Tourneur to explain apparent differences which he sees, clearly enough, between the two plays at issue – but the biography depends on the initial assumption, and Jenkins is arguing in a circle.

Two other defenders of Tourneur's claim remain to be considered, both more elusive than those so far mentioned.

10 R.H. Barker, *Thomas Middleton* (Columbia University Press, 1958); Schoenbaum, *Middleton's Tragedies*.

11 H.D. Sykes, *Sidelights on Elizabethan Drama* (Oxford University Press, 1924), p. 211; U. Ellis Fermor, 'The imagery of *The Revenger's Tragedy* and *The Atheist's Tragedy*', *M.L.R.* XXX (1935), p. 289f.; Foakes, 'On the authorship', p. 129f.

12 Inga-Stina Ekblad, 'An approach to Tourneur's imagery', *M.L.R.* LIV (1959), p. 489f.

Foakes[13] does a good job of negative criticism on the Middletonians, doing real damage to the case based on statistics, questioning the Keysar 'link', harming the arguments which draw on similarity of character-naming – yet his conclusion has a faint air of hopelessness: 'the plays show a marked development in thought and seem remarkably alike in the more intangible qualities which evade strict analysis, in mood, general temper and moral fervour'. Unfortunately attribution calls for 'strict analysis', and 'intangible qualities' will convince no one who does not share Foakes's subjective belief. I do not mean that one's 'feeling' for common authorship is necessarily wrong, but argument from this can hardly proceed beyond H.D. Sykes and, in any case, my own apprehension of 'mood, general temper and moral fervour' in these two plays is quite unlike that of Professor Foakes. The same trouble arises with Irving Ribner, whose main defect as a critic is to see literature as moral tract. An ability to see *The Revenger's Tragedy* as having a 'crusading missionary tone' depends upon providing the play with a context which it does not, of itself, summon up – whereas *The Atheist's Tragedy* drags such a Christian context unrelentingly in. So when Ribner concludes that the latter play 'exhibits little progress in aesthetic range, but . . . is remarkably like [*The Revenger's Tragedy*] in its moral and religious point of view'[14] one is led to comment that Ribner's confidence might be shaken if he were more responsive to 'aesthetic range' and if he were more aware of the dangers of importing contexts for works of art – shades of Hamlet's father's ghost walk the pages of Ribner's discussion and the issue of the 'guilt' of Webster's Duchess of Malfi might provide another lesson.

The positive case for Tourneur's authorship of *The Revenger's Tragedy*, then, seems to be fairly weak, even if strong enough to cast doubts on the case for Middleton. Similarities of theme need to be examined critically before they are accepted as evidence of common authorship: are the common themes usual ones in the drama of the time, in substance and/or treatment? Are these themes treated in such a way as to preclude the possibility that two minds worked on a common body of traditional material? Can we rule out the possibility of *The Atheist's Tragedy* being an answer by one dramatist to the earlier challenge of another writer in *The*

13 Foakes, 'On the authorship', p. 129f.
14 Ribner, *The Atheist's Tragedy*, pp. 72, 95.

Revenger's Tragedy? I do not think that any of these questions has really been adequately dealt with – and, unless they are, the case for Tourneur is hardly a case at all, but rather a 'feeling'.

The only serious alternative known dramatist as author of *The Revenger's Tragedy* is, as indicated, Thomas Middleton. The main basis for his claim has been statistical and has been developed chiefly by G.R. Price and, more elaborately, by P.B. Murray.[15] Murray's case is closely argued and backed up by a formidable array of statistics – but Murray is his own best critic, even if a rather muddled one. In the preface to his *Study of Cyril Tourneur* he says, referring to his essay of 1962, 'My study of *The Revenger's Tragedy* has turned up new and I think conclusive internal evidence that Thomas Middleton is the author' (p. 7). In his book he reprints his essay, but then (p. 173) adds, 'Although the evidence strongly supports Middleton's claim to *The Revenger's Tragedy*, the tests I have used leave a slight chance that Tourneur is the author. So long as we study this problem at least one remove from the author's papers, we can never do more than establish a *probability* of authorship by means of linguistic and spelling tests, and that probability is only as good as the inferences about scribes and compositors will allow. Moreover, other statistical analyses than those I have made will yield different degrees of certainty for assignment of the play to Middleton, some of them no doubt less than that I have shown.'

So Murray finishes up in a position far from the certainty he had earlier had, and, if the statistical evidence fails to establish anything like the level of probability Murray once claimed, much of the case for Middleton collapses. It is true that claims have been made on other grounds. W.D. Dunkel[16] managed to touch on most of them in his essay, but none of them is more than possible supporting evidence for a case that has to be primarily based on something else. Dunkel's verbal parallels, for instance, are invalidated in that some are vague, some are mere commonplaces, and that he fails to use negative checks or to consider the possibility of imitation. His arguments about the opening speech in *The Revenger's Tragedy* and the play's use

15 G.R. Price, 'The authorship and the bibliography of *The Revenger's Tragedy*', *The Library*, 5th series, XV (1960); P.B. Murray 'The authorship of *The Revenger's Tragedy*', *Papers of the Bibliographical Society of America*, LVI (1962).

16 'The authorship of *The Revenger's Tragedy*', *P.M.L.A.* XLVI (1931).

of disguise also fail to take adequate account of the practices of other dramatists than Middleton (notably Jonson and Marston) and of that common sport of Jacobean dramatists – imitation. None of the attempts to make a case for Middleton seems to ring true, for none has a wide enough base, none pays enough attention to the broad field of Jacobean drama. If one takes into account the accumulated evidence of the dramatic background to the play (see above) there is little left of the Middleton case except the substylistic one which Murray developed and then came to doubt.[17]

The situation we are left in after looking at the attribution question is not very satisfactory. It is not easy to accept that *The Revenger's Tragedy* is the only play of its author, an author, clearly, of outstanding talent. It is tempting to treat it as Tourneur's because there are interesting parallels of material, and interesting differences of treatment in the two plays printed in this volume – but it is also tempting to assign it to Middleton so that one can re-examine that dramatist's achievement with *The Revenger's Tragedy* in mind. But unless new evidence emerges – preferably external; if internal, by way of new sophistication of stylistic and substylistic analysis – the play has to be regarded as anonymous. To give it to either Tourneur or Middleton, at the present state of play, would be irresponsible in the light of the arguments and evidence so far brought forward. It seems to me that we are not really even in a position to rule out the possibility that *The Revenger's Tragedy* is the work of a known dramatist other than Tourneur or Middleton, if we remember the versatility of most major Jacobean writers.

17 David Lake (*The Canon of Thomas Middleton's Plays*, Cambridge, 1975) has recently extended the work of earlier scholars on the statistical analysis of *The Revenger's Tragedy* in relation to other plays, his view being 'that the conclusion by now must be almost irresistible that the copy for the substantive early quarto was a Middleton holograph' (p. 136). Lake's analysis certainly strengthens the case for Middleton, but he pays little heed to other sorts of evidence (especially concerning ways of thought and dramatic technique) which throw doubt on conclusions reached through stylistic examination.

THE REVENGERS TRAGÆDIE.

As it hath beene sundry times Acted, by the Kings Maiesties Seruants.

AT LONDON.
Printed by G. Eld, and are to be sold at his house in Fleete-lane at the signe of the Printers-Presse.
1607.

Title-page of the 1607 Quarto of *The Revenger's Tragedy*, reproduced by permission of the British Library.

INTRODUCTORY NOTE

Sources

One of the unusual characteristics of *The Revenger's Tragedy* is that nothing that can be called a source for its plot has been found. This, of course, is not the same thing as saying that none exists or has existed, but it seems probable that this is the case. On the other hand it would be wrong to conclude from this that the play is, in the literal sense, original. In fact, evidence has accumulated over the years that the play is 'synthetic', its originality a matter of the tone and final shape of the synthesis. Three categories of material need to be considered.

In the first place there is some evidence of sources for particular strands in the play's plot. G.K. Hunter has shown that the incident in which Lussurioso enters his parents' bedchamber expecting to find his mother in bed with Spurio has its source in the *Aethiopian History* of Heliodorus (which had been translated by Underdowne in 1587), while in Margaret of Navarre's *Heptameron* there is a story (XII) which may well provide the source for the Lussurioso–Vindice–Castiza plot-motif. The story was available in English in Painter's popular *Palace of Pleasure*: the dramatist, whether he used Painter or Margaret's original text, has altered the tone considerably, and the circumstances which surround the plot-thread differ in the two cases. Ross has suggested that the rape of Antonio's wife and the subsequent revenge by certain lords may have been based on the widely known story of the rape of Lucrece.[1]

Secondly, we need to take account of a body of material which is scarcely source material in the orthodox sense but which seems to have influenced the dramatist's attitude to his material: I am thinking here of the arguments put forward by Peter, Salingar, Schoenbaum and Higgins to the effect that the author of *The Revenger's Tragedy* was aware of traditional literary and iconographic material concerning such themes as the dance of death and such literary forms as 'complaint' and the morality plays.[2] I think that this context has, as these writers argue, undoubtedly helped to shape this play, but it is perhaps worth making the point that this is not, in itself, evidence that the dramatist has the same moral view of his

1 G.K. Hunter, 'A source for *The Revenger's Tragedy*', *R.E.S.* X (1959); L.J. Ross (ed.) *The Revenger's Tragedy* (London: Regents Renaissance Drama Series, 1966), p. 19.

2 Peter, *Complaint and satire*; Salingar, 'The morality tradition'; Schoenbaum, 'Jacobean dance of death'; Higgins, 'The influence of Calvinist thought'.

material as is present in the traditions in question – one has only to remember Jonson's use of morality tradition (or even Marlowe's) to realise that awareness of tradition and subservience to it need not go hand in hand.

Thirdly, there is the important evidence of this dramatist's use of motifs and attitudes from other plays of the period. It is not possible to look in any detail at this here: an example or two will have to suffice. Marston's use of sensational revenge situations in the *Antonio* plays seems to lie behind the shaping of the revenge theme in *The Revenger's Tragedy*, and it is important to remember that behind Marston lies much of the revenge drama initiated by Kyd, notably *The Jew of Malta*, *Hoffman*, and *Hamlet*. The satirical tone and detail of the play remind a reader of Ben Jonson, particularly the Jonson of *Volpone*, which shares the bleakness of *The Revenger's Tragedy* world.

These and other influences are drawn together in this play, but none, I think, is allowed to dominate it and all are subordinate to the total effect. Here again one is reminded most of Jonson: he also was a great synthesiser and he too was a master at uniting a variety of material into a fully coherent whole.

Stage-history

It has already been pointed out that there is no independent evidence to support the claim on the title-page of the first edition that *The Revenger's Tragedy* had been acted 'sundry times . . . by the King Majesties Servants'. The absence of such evidence does not prove that the play was not acted, and it would be surprising if it remained unperformed in the early seventeenth century. Until recent years, however, there is nothing we can call a stage-history, but the productions at Stratford and at the Pitlochry Festival brought the play to the attention of many who might not otherwise have known it, and also showed that it is, although difficult, a play that can be produced effectively in our time – if the producer has the confidence to trust the dramatist's strange and disturbing mixture of horror and farce.

A note on editions

Although the practice of editing *The Revenger's Tragedy* by itself is relatively recent it is necessary to mention in passing the Tourneur editions of Collins (1873) and Symonds (1893). Collins printed the play in his *Plays and Poems of Cyril Tourneur* and the carelessness of his text was perpetuated in Symonds's *Mermaid* volume, which is still around and which has hampered a number of critics who unwisely assumed its accuracy. There is now little need for this sort of error, since several modern editions have appeared, by Gibbons (New Mermaids, 1967), L.J. Ross (Regents Renaissance Drama Series, 1966) and R.A. Foakes (Revels Plays, 1966). Gibbons's text is occasionally suspect and his annotation rather light, but the critical section of his introduction is stimulating and makes good use of illustrations to point up the traditional background to the play. Ross, like Gibbons and Foakes, presents a modernised text: his text is more reliable than that of Gibbons and the annotation fuller, but the introduction is pedestrian. Foakes provides a good text, full annotation and a thorough introduction. One should also mention that the Scolar Press are proposing to issue a facsimile of the first edition in the near future.

DRAMATIS PERSONAE

THE DUKE
LUSSURIOSO, the duke's son
SPURIO, the bastard
AMBITIOSO, the duchess's eldest son
SUPERVACUO, the duchess's second son
YOUNGEST SON of the duchess
VINDICE, a revenger (also, in disguise, called PIATO) } brothers to Castiza
HIPPOLITO, also called CARLO }
ANTONIO } nobles
PIERO }
DONDOLO
THE DUCHESS
CASTIZA
GRATIANA, mother of Castiza
Nobles
Judges
Gentlemen
Officers
Keeper
Servants

Lussurioso	luxurious (i.e. lecherous)
Ambitioso	ambitious
Supervacuo	foolish
Piato	here 'covered', 'disguised'
Castiza	chastity
Gratiana	grace

THE REVENGER'S TRAGEDY

ACT I

SCENE I

Enter VINDICE. *The* DUKE, DUCHESS, LUSSURIOSO *his son,* SPURIO *the bastard, with a train, pass over the stage with torchlight.*

VINDICE. Duke, royal lecher! Go, grey-haired adultery,
And thou his son, as impious steeped as he,
And thou his bastard true-begot in evil,
And thou his duchess that will do with devil:
Four exc'lent characters! O, that marrowless age
Would stuff the hollow bones with damned desires,
And 'stead of heat kindle infernal fires
Within the spendthrift veins of a dry duke,
A parched and juiceless luxur. O God! One
That has scarce blood enough to live upon,
And he to riot it like a son and heir?
O the thought of that
Turns my abusèd heartstrings into fret. –
(*To the skull he is carrying*) Thou sallow picture of my poisoned love,
My study's ornament, thou shell of death,
Once the bright face of my betrothed lady,
When life and beauty naturally filled out
These ragged imperfections,
When two heaven-pointed diamonds were set
In those unsightly rings – then 'twas a face
So far beyond the artificial shine
Of any woman's bought complexion
That the uprightest man (if such there be
That sin but seven times a day) broke custom
And made up eight with looking after her.
O she was able to ha'made a usurer's son

---

2 *his*: see Textual note, p. 195.
4 *do*: in the sexual sense.
5 *characters*: examples of particular types of humanity.
6 *Would*: some editors follow Dodsley in amending to 'Should' but this is not strictly necessary.
9 *luxur*: lecher.
13 *fret*: (a) distress, turbulence; (b) a small wooden or metal bridge set across the finger board of a stringed instrument.

Melt all his patrimony in a kiss,
And what his father fifty years told
To have consumed, and yet his suit been cold.
But, O accursed palace!
Thee, when thou wert apparelled in thy flesh,
The old duke poisoned
Because thy purer part would not consent
Unto his palsy-lust; for old men lustful
Do show like young men angry, eager-violent,
Outbid like their limited performances.
O, 'ware an old man hot and vicious:
'Age as in gold, in lust is covetous.' –
Vengeance, thou murder's quit-rent, and whereby
Thou show'st thyself tenant to tragedy,
O keep thy day, hour, minute, I beseech,
For those thou hast determined. Hum! Who e'er knew
Murder unpaid? Faith, give Revenge her due,
Sh'as kept touch hitherto. – Be merry, merry;
Advance thee, O thou terror to fat folks,
To have their costly three-piled flesh worn off
As bare as this, for banquets, ease and laughter
Can make great men, as greatness goes by clay,
But wise men little are more great than they!

Enter his brother HIPPOLITO.

HIPPOLITO. Still sighing o'er death's vizard?
VINDICE. Brother, welcome!
What comfort bring'st thou? How go things at court?
HIPPOLITO. In silk and silver, brother, never braver.
VINDICE. Pooh,
Thou play'st upon my meaning: prithee say

---

27 *patrimony*: wealth inherited from the father.
28 *told*: accumulated, added up.
29 *his . . . cold*: his wooing have been in vain.
37 *vicious*: inclined to vice.
39 *quit-rent*: the rent a freeholder pays his lord for exemption from dues of service: the idea here is that vengeance is murder's due.
42 *determined*: fixed inexorably.
44 *kept touch*: remained faithful.
46 *three-piled*: the most luxurious kind of velvet.
50 *vizard*: mask.
52 *braver*: more ostentatiously.

Has that bald madam, Opportunity,
Yet thought upon's? Speak, are we happy yet?
Thy wrongs and mine are for one scabbard fit.
HIPPOLITO. It may prove happiness.
VINDICE. What is't may prove?
Give me to taste.
HIPPOLITO. Give me your hearing then.
You know my place at court?
VINDICE. Ay, the duke's chamber –
But 'tis a marvel thou'rt not turned out yet.
HIPPOLITO. Faith, I have been shoved at, but 'twas still my hap
To hold by th'duchess' skirt: you guess at that –
Whom such a coat keeps up can ne'er fall flat.
But to the purpose.
Last evening, predecessor unto this,
The duke's son warily enquired for me,
Whose pleasure I attended. He began
By policy to open and unhusk me
About the time and common rumour,
But I had so much wit to keep my thoughts
Up in their built houses, yet afforded him
An idle satisfaction without danger.
But the whole aim and scope of his intent
Ended in this: conjuring me in private
To seek some strange-digested fellow forth
Of ill-contented nature, either disgraced
In former times, or by new grooms displaced
Since his stepmother's nuptials; such a blood,
A man that were for evil only good:
To give you the true word, some base-coined pandar.
VINDICE. I reach you, for I know his heat is such,
Were there as many concubines as ladies
He would not be contained; he must fly out.

---

55 *Opportunity* (= *Occasion* at l. 98) was, in Renaissance iconography, a bald, winged female with a single forelock.

62 *hap*: good fortune.

72 *built houses*: i.e. in the sections of the brain set aside for them (there may be an echo here of the 'memory theatres' discussed by Frances Yates in *The Art of Memory* (Routledge and Kegan Paul, 1966)).

76 *strange-digested*: oddly disposed.

81 *base-coined*: low-born.

I wonder how ill-featured, vild-proportioned
That one should be, if she were made for woman,
Whom at the insurrection of his lust
He would refuse for once: heart, I think none.
Next to a skull, though more unsound than one,
Each face he meets he strongly dotes upon.

HIPPOLITO. Brother, y'ave truly spoke him.
He knows not you, but I'll swear you know him.

VINDICE. And therefore I'll put on that knave for once
And be a right man then, a man o'th'time;
For to be honest is not to be i'th'world.

HIPPOLITO. And I'll prefer you, brother.

VINDICE. Go to, then.
The small'st advantage fattens wrongèd men.
It may point out Occasion; if I meet her
I'll hold her by the foretop fast enough,
Or like the French mole heave up hair and all.
I have a habit that will fit it quaintly.

Enter GRATIANA *and* CASTIZA.

Here comes our mother.

HIPPOLITO. And sister.

VINDICE. We must coin.
Women are apt you know to take false money;
But I dare stake my soul for these two creatures;
Only excuse excepted, that they'll swallow
Because their sex is easy in belief.

GRATIANA. What news from court, son Carlo?

HIPPOLITO. Faith, mother,
'Tis whispered there the duchess' youngest son
Has played a rape on lord Antonio's wife.

GRATIANA. On that religious lady!

CASTIZA. Royal blood: monster! He deserves to die,

---

85 *vild-*: vile-
87 *insurrection*: onset, rising up.
94 *right*: conventional.
96 *prefer*: put you forward for recognition; favour.
98–9 See note to I.i.55; 'foretop' = 'forelock'.
100 A mole damages grass: the 'French mole' here = syphilis, which causes hair to drop out.
101 *quaintly*: exactly, cleverly.
102 *coin*: dissimulate.
104 *stake*: gamble on.

If Italy had no more hopes but he.
VINDICE. Sister, y'ave sentenced most direct and true:
The law's a woman, and would she were you. –
Mother, I must take leave of you.
GRATIANA. Leave for what?
VINDICE. I intend speedy travel.
HIPPOLITO. That he does, madam.
GRATIANA. Speedy indeed!
VINDICE. For since my worthy father's funeral
My life's unnaturally to me, e'en compelled
As if I lived now when I should be dead.
GRATIANA. Indeed he was a worthy gentleman,
Had his estate been fellow to his mind.
VINDICE. The duke did much deject him.
GRATIANA. Much!
VINDICE. Too much.
And through disgrace oft smothered in his spirit
When it would mount: surely I think he died
Of discontent, the nobleman's consumption.
GRATIANA. Most sure he did.
VINDICE. Did he? 'Lack, you know all,
You were his midnight secretary.
GRATIANA. No.
He was too wise to trust me with his thoughts.
VINDICE. (*aside*) I'faith then, father, thou wast wise indeed:
'Wives are but made to go to bed and feed.' –
Come mother, sister – you'll bring me onward brother?
HIPPOLITO. I will.
VINDICE. (*aside*) I'll quickly turn into another.
Exeunt all.

SCENE II

Enter the old DUKE, LUSSURIOSO *his son, the* DUCHESS, SPURIO *the bastard, the duchess's two sons* AMBITIOSO *and* SUPERVACUO, *the*

---

114 *the law's a woman*: Justice was often imaged as a female figure holding scales or a sword.
116 *travel*: with a pun on 'travail' (labour). Q. has 'travail': the two spellings are commonly interchangeable at this time.
123 *deject*: neglect, keep him poor.
128 *secretary*: confidant.

third – her YOUNGEST SON – *brought out with officers for trial for the rape, two judges.*

DUKE. Duchess, it is your youngest son; we're sorry
His violent act has e'en drawn blood of honour
And stained our honours,
Thrown ink upon the forehead of our state
Which envious spirits will dip their pens into
After our death, and blot us in our tombs.
For that which would seem treason in our lives
Is laughter when we're dead. Who dares now whisper
That dares not then speak out, and e'en proclaim
With loud words and broad pens our closest shame?
FIRST JUDGE. Your grace hath spoken like to your silver years,
Full of confirmed gravity; for what is it to have
A flattering false insculption on a tomb
And in men's hearts reproach? The boweled corpse
May be cered in, but, with free tongue I speak,
'The faults of great men through their cerecloths break.'
DUKE. They do, we're sorry for't; it is our fate
To live in fear and die to live in hate.
I leave him to your sentence: doom him lords –
The fact is great – whilst I sit by and sigh.
DUCHESS. (*kneeling*) My gracious lord, I pray be merciful
Although his trespass far exceed his years.
Think him to be your own as I am yours,
Call him not son-in-law: the law I fear
Will fall too soon upon his name and him.
Temper his fault with pity!
LUSSURIOSO. Good my lord,
Then 'twill not taste so bitter and unpleasant
Upon the judges' palate; for offences
Gilt o'er with mercy show like fairest women,
Good only for their beauties, which, washed off
No sin is uglier.

---

10 *broad pens*: frank and/or scurrilous writings.
12 *confirmed*: mature, fully fixed.
13 *insculption*: inscription.
14 *boweled*: disemboweled.
15 *cered in*: wrapped in cerecloths (waxed sheets).
26 *Temper*: mitigate.

AMBITIOSO. I beseech your grace
Be soft and mild, let not relentless law
Look with an iron forehead on our brother.
SPURIO. (*aside*) He yields small comfort yet, hope he shall die;
And if a bastard's wish might stand in force,
Would all the court were turned into a corse.
DUCHESS. No pity yet? Must I rise fruitless then?
A wonder in a woman! Are my knees
Of such low metal that without respect –
FIRST JUDGE. Let the offender stand forth:
'Tis the duke's pleasure that impartial doom
Shall take first hold of his unclean attempt.
A rape! Why 'tis the very core of lust,
Double adultery.
YOUNGEST SON. So, sir.
SECOND JUDGE. And which was worse,
Committed on the lord Antonio's wife,
That general honest lady. Confess, my lord,
What moved you to't?
YOUNGEST SON. Why, flesh and blood, my lord.
What should move men unto a woman else?
LUSSURIOSO. O do not jest thy doom, trust not an axe
Or sword too far: the law is a wise serpent
And quickly can beguile thee of thy life.
Though marriage only has made thee my brother
I love thee so far: play not with thy death.
YOUNGEST SON. I thank you, troth; good admonitions, faith,
If I'd the grace now to make use of them.
FIRST JUDGE. That lady's name has spread such a fair wing
Over all Italy that if our tongues
Were sparing toward the fact, judgement itself
Would be condemned and suffer in men's thoughts.
YOUNGEST SON. Well then, 'tis done, and it would please me well
Were it to do again: sure she's a goddess,
For I'd no power to see her and to live.

---

36 *corse*: corpse.
42 *first*: see Textual note, p. 195.
46 *general honest*: honest in all respects.

It falls out true in this, for I must die;
Her beauty was ordained to be my scaffold,
And yet, methinks, I might be easier ceased:
My fault being sport, let me but die in jest.

FIRST JUDGE. This be the sentence –

DUCHESS. O keep't upon your tongue, let it not slip:
Death too soon steals out of a lawyer's lip.
Be not so cruel-wise!

FIRST JUDGE. Your grace must pardon us,
'Tis but the justice of the law.

DUCHESS. The law
Is grown more subtle than a woman should be.

SPURIO. (*aside*) Now, now he dies; rid 'em away.

DUCHESS. (*aside*) O what it is to have an old-cool duke
To be as slack in tongue as in performance.

FIRST JUDGE. Confirmed, this be the doom irrevocable.

DUCHESS. O!

FIRST JUDGE. Tomorrow early –

DUCHESS. Pray be abed, my lord.

FIRST JUDGE. Your grace much wrongs yourself.

AMBITIOSO. No, 'tis that tongue,
Your too much right does do us too much wrong.

FIRST JUDGE. Let that offender –

DUCHESS. Live, and be in health.

FIRST JUDGE. Be on a scaffold –

DUKE. Hold, hold, my lord!

SPURIO. (*aside*) Pox on't,
What makes my dad speak now?

DUKE. We will defer the judgement till next sitting;
In the meantime let him be kept close prisoner:
Guard, bear him hence.

AMBITIOSO. (*to Youngest Son*) Brother, this makes for thee;
Fear not, we'll have a trick to set thee free.

YOUNGEST SON. Brother, I will expect it from you both,
And in that hope I rest.

SUPERVACUO. Farewell, be merry.

Exit YOUNGEST SON *with a guard.*

---

65 *ceased*: see Textual note, p. 195.
75 *performance*: sexual prowess.
81 *Pox*: see Textual note, p. 195.
85 *makes for thee*: is to your advantage.
87–8 See Textual note, p. 195.

SPURIO. (*aside*) Delayed, deferred! Nay then if judgement have
Cold blood flattery and bribes will kill it.
DUKE. About it then, my lords, with your best powers:
More serious business calls upon our hours.
Exeunt all except the DUCHESS.
DUCHESS. Was't ever known step-duchess was so mild
And calm as I? Some now would plot his death
With easy doctors, those loose-living men,
And make his withered grace fall to his grave
And keep church better.
Some second wife would do this, and dispatch
Her double-loathèd lord at meat and sleep.
Indeed 'tis true an old man's twice a child:
Mine cannot speak; one of his single words
Would quite have freed my youngest, dearest son
From death or durance, and have made him walk
With a bold foot upon the thorny law,
Whose prickles should bow under him. But 'tis not,
And therefore wedlock faith shall be forgot.
I'll kill him in his forehead; hate, there feed:
That wound is deepest though it never bleed.
And here comes he whom my heart points unto,
His bastard son, but my love's true-begot;

Enter SPURIO.

Many a wealthy letter have I sent him
Swelled up with jewels, and the timorous man
Is yet but coldly kind.
That jewel's mine that quivers in his ear,
Mocking his master's chillness and vain fear –
H'as spied me now.
SPURIO. Madam, your grace so private?
My duty on your hand.
DUCHESS. Upon my hand, sir. Troth, I think you'd fear
To kiss my hand too if my lip stood there.
SPURIO. Witness I would not, madam. *Kisses her.*

---

97 i.e. the duke, buried in church, would be a more regular attender there than in life.
101 *one . . . words*: a single word.
103 *durance*: imprisonment.
107 *kill . . . forehead*: destroy him by committing adultery (the reference is to the horns of a cuckold).

DUCHESS. 'Tis a wonder,
For ceremony has made many fools.
It is as easy way unto a duchess
As to a hatted dame, if her love answer,
But that by timorous honours, pale respects,
Idle degrees of fear, men make their ways
Hard of themselves. What have you thought of me?
SPURIO. Madam, I ever think of you in duty,
Regard and –
DUCHESS. Pooh! Upon my love, I mean.
SPURIO. I would 'twere love, but 'tas a fouler name
Than lust: you are my father's wife:
Your grace may guess now what I could call it.
DUCHESS. Why th'art his son but falsely;
'Tis a hard question whether he begot thee.
SPURIO. I'faith, 'tis true too; I'm an uncertain man
Of more uncertain woman. May be his groom
O'th'stable begot me; you know I know not.
He could ride a horse well; a shrewd suspicion, marry!
He was wondrous tall; he had his length, i'faith,
For peeping over half-shut holiday windows:
Men would desire him 'light. When he was afoot
He made a goodly show under a pent-house;
And when he rid his hat would check the signs
And clatter barbers' basins.
DUCHESS. Nay, set you a-horseback once
You'll ne'er 'light off.
SPURIO. Indeed I am a beggar.
DUCHESS. That's more the sign thou'rt great. – But to our love:

---

123 *hatted dame*: hats seem to have been worn mainly by the lower classes.
answer: responds.

135–9 See Textual note, p. 195.

139 *half-shut holiday windows*: presumably windows half-shut because people were resting on holidays.

142 *check*: strike.

143 *barbers' basins*: often used as shop-signs.

144 M.P. Tilley, *A Dictionary of Proverbs in England in the Sixteenth and Seventeenth Centuries* (Ann Arbor, 1950), has the proverb 'Set a beggar on horseback he will ride a gallop' (Spurio and the duchess are using the idea sexually).

Let it stand firm, both in thought and mind,
That the duke was thy father, as no doubt then
He bid fair for't: thy injury is the more;
For had he cut thee a right diamond
Thou hadst been next set in the dukedom's ring,
When his worn self, like age's easy slave,
Had dropped out of the collet into the grave.
What wrong can equal this? Canst thou be tame
And think upon't?

SPURIO. No, mad and think upon't.

DUCHESS. Who would not be revenged of such a father,
E'en in the worst way? I would thank that sin
That could most injury him, and be in league with it.
O what a grief 'tis that a man should live
But once i'th'world, and then to live a bastard,
The curse o'the womb, the thief of nature,
Begot against the seventh commandément,
Half-damned in the conception by the justice
Of that unbribèd, everlasting law.

SPURIO. O, I'd a hot-backed devil to my father.

DUCHESS. Would not this mad e'en patience, make blood rough?
Who but an eunuch would not sin, his bed
By one false minute disinherited?

SPURIO. Ay, there's the vengeance that my birth was wrapped in!
I'll be revenged for all. Now hate begin;
I'll call incest but a venial sin.

DUCHESS. Cold still: in vain then must a duchess woo?

SPURIO. Madam, I blush to say what I will do.

DUCHESS. Thence flew sweet comfort. Earnest and farewell. *She kisses him.*

SPURIO. O, one incestuous kiss picks open hell.

DUCHESS. Faith, now, old duke, my vengeance shall reach high:
I'll arm thy brow with woman's heraldry.

Exit the DUCHESS.

---

152 *collet*: setting for a jewel.
161 *commandément*: see Textual note, p. 195.
164 *hot-backed*: lecherous.
170 *venial*: pardonable.
173 *Earnest*: i.e. the kiss is a promise of more in the future.
176 *woman's heraldry*: i.e. cuckold's horns.

SPURIO. Duke, thou didst me wrong, and by that act
Adultery is my nature.
Faith, if the truth were known, I was begot
After some gluttonous dinner, some stirring dish
Was my first father: when deep healths went round
And ladies' cheeks were painted red with wine,
Their tongues, as short and nimble as their heels,
Uttering words sweet and thick; and when they rose,
Were merrily disposed to fall again.
In such a whisp'ring and withdrawing hour,
When base male bawds kept sentinel at stair-head,
Was I stol'n softly. O, damnation met
The sin of feasts, drunken adultery:
I feel it swell me; my revenge is just:
I was begot in impudent wine and lust.
Stepmother, I consent to thy desires;
I love thy mischief well but I hate thee
And those three cubs, thy sons, wishing confusion,
Death and disgrace may be their epitaphs.
As for my brother, the duke's only son,
Whose birth is more beholding to report
Than mine, and yet perhaps as falsely sown
(Women must not be trusted with their own),
I'll loose my days upon him, hate-all I.
Duke, on thy brow I'll draw my bastardy.
For indeed a bastard by nature should make cuckolds
Because he is the son of a cuckold-maker. *Exit* SPURIO.

SCENE III

Enter VINDICE *and* HIPPOLITO (VINDICE *in disguise as* PIATO) *to attend* LUSSURIOSO *the duke's son.*

VINDICE. What, brother, am I far enough from myself?
HIPPOLITO. As if another man had been sent whole
Into the world and none wist how he came.

---

180 *stirring*: stimulating.
197–8 *birth . . . mine*: whose birth is, in people's eyes, more respectable than mine.
200 *loose my days*: devote my time to vengeance.
1 *am . . . myself*: i.e. am I well enough disguised?
3 *wist*: knew.

VINDICE. It will confirm me bold: the child o'th'court;
Let blushes dwell i'th'country. Impudence,
Thou goddess of the palace, mistress of mistresses,
To whom the costly-perfumed people pray,
Strike thou my forehead into dauntless marble,
Mine eyes to steady sapphires; turn my visage,
And if I must needs glow let me blush inward
That this immodest season may not spy
That scholar in my cheeks, fool bashfulness,
That maid in the old time whose flush of grace
Would never suffer her to get good clothes.
Our maids are wiser and are less ashamed;
Save Grace the bawd I seldom hear grace named!

HIPPOLITO. Nay, brother, you reach out o'th'verge now. –

Enter LUSSURIOSO *attended.*

'Sfoot, the duke's son! Settle your looks.

VINDICE. Pray let me not be doubted.

HIPPOLITO. My lord.

LUSSURIOSO. Hippolito? (*To servants*) Be absent, leave us.

Exeunt servants.

HIPPOLITO. My lord, after long search, wary enquiries
And politic siftings, I made choice of yon fellow
Whom I guess rare for many deep employments.
This our age swims within him; and if Time
Had so much hair I should take him for Time,
He is so near kin to this present minute.

LUSSURIOSO. 'Tis enough,
We thank thee: yet words are but great men's blanks;
Gold, though it be dumb, does utter the best thanks.

Gives him money.

13–14 Nakedness signified innocence and truth (with an obvious connection with the prelapsarian state) and emblems often presented these qualities as nude personifications.

16 *Grace the bawd*: Nicoll sees a possible contemporary reference here. More important is the ironic foreshadowing of the role of Gratiana (= Grace).

17–18 See Textual note, p. 195.

19 *doubted*: suspected.

28 *blanks*: Harrison suggests a reference to lottery tickets which miss the prizes; Foakes to metal shaped for coins but not yet value-stamped.

HIPPOLITO. Your plenteous honour. – An exc'lent fellow,
my lord.
LUSSURIOSO. So, give us leave.
Exit HIPPOLITO.
Welcome, be not far off,
We must be better acquainted. Push, be bold
With us: thy hand.
VINDICE. With all my heart, i'faith!
How dost, sweet muskcat? When shall we lie together?
LUSSURIOSO. (*aside*) Wondrous knave!
Gather him into boldness; 'sfoot, the slave's
Already as familiar as an ague
And shakes me at his pleasure. – Friend, I can
Forget myself in private, but elsewhere
I pray do you remember me.
VINDICE. O very well, sir.
I conster myself saucy.
LUSSURIOSO. What hast been?
Of what profession?
VINDICE. A bone-setter.
LUSSURIOSO. A bone-setter!
VINDICE. A bawd, my lord:
One that sets bones together.
LUSSURIOSO. Notable bluntness! –
(*Aside*) Fit, fit for me, e'en trained up to my hand. –
Thou hast been scrivener to much knavery then?
VINDICE. Fool to abundance, sir: I have been witness
To the surrenders of a thousand virgins,
And not so little;
I have seen patrimonies washed a-pieces,
Fruit fields turned into bastards,
And in a world of acres
Not so much dust due to the heir 'twas left to
As would well gravel a petition.
LUSSURIOSO. (*aside*) Fine villain! 'Troth, I like him
wondrously;
He's e'en shaped for my purpose. – Then thou know'st

31–4 See Textual note, p. 195.
34 *muskcat*: literally, musk-deer; figuratively, fop or prostitute.
40 *remember me*: remember who I am.
41 *conster*: construe, consider.
46 *scrivener*: agent for.
54 *gravel*: blot (sand was often used to dry ink).

I'th'world strange lust?
VINDICE. O Dutch lust! Fulsome lust!
Drunken procreation, which begets so many drunkards.
Some father dreads not (gone to bed in wine) to slide
From the mother, and cling the daughter-in-law;
Some uncles are adulterous with their nieces,
Brothers with brothers' wives: O hour of incest!
Any kin now, next to the rim o'th'sister,
Is man's meat in these days, and in the morning,
When they are up and dressed and their mask on,
Who can perceive this save that eternal eye
That sees through flesh and all? Well, if any thing
Be damned it will be twelve o'clock at night;
That twelve will never 'scape;
It is the Judas of the hours, wherein
Honest salvation is betrayed to sin.
LUSSURIOSO. In troth it is too. But let this talk glide.
It is our blood to err, though hell gaped loud;
Ladies know Lucifer fell, yet still are proud.
Now, sir, wert thou as secret as thou'rt subtle
And deeply fathomed into all estates,
I would embrace thee for a near employment,
And thou shouldst swell in money, and be able
To make lame beggars crouch to thee.
VINDICE. My lord!
Secret? I ne'er had that disease o'th'mother,
I praise my father. Why are men made close
But to keep thoughts in best? I grant you this:
Tell but some woman a secret overnight,
Your doctor may find it in the urinal i'th'morning;
But, my lord –
LUSSURIOSO. So, thou'rt confirmed in me,
And thus I enter thee. *Gives* VINDICE *money.*
VINDICE. This Indian devil

---

57 *Dutch lust*: as the Dutch were considered heavy drinkers this phrase = Drunken procreation in l. 58.
60 *cling*: embrace.
63 *rim*: (a) limit; (b) vagina.
72 *glide*: be passed over.
76 *estates*: types of people.
80 *disease . . . mother*: i.e. of talking too much.
85 *confirmed in me*: established in my confidence.
86 *Indian devil*: the Indies were seen as the treasury of gold and silver.

Will quickly enter any man but a usurer:
He prevents that by ent'ring the devil first.
LUSSURIOSO. Attend me. I am past my depth in lust
And I must swim or drown. All my desires
Are levelled at a virgin not far from court,
To whom I have conveyed by messenger
Many waxed lines full of my neatest spirits
And jewels that were able to ravish her
Without the help of man: all which and more
She, foolish-chaste, sent back, the messengers
Receiving frowns for answers.
VINDICE. Possible?
'Tis a rare phoenix, whosoe'er she be;
If your desires be such, she so repugnant,
In troth, my lord, I'd be revenged and marry her.
LUSSURIOSO. Push! The dowry of her blood and of her fortunes
Are both too mean – good enough to be bad withal.
I'm one of that number can defend
Marriage is good, yet rather keep a friend.
Give me my bed by stealth – there's true delight;
What breeds a loathing in't, but night by night?
VINDICE. A very fine religion!
LUSSURIOSO. Therefore thus:
I'll trust thee in the business of my heart
Because I see thee well experienced
In this luxurious day wherein we breathe.
Go thou and with a smooth, enchanting tongue
Bewitch her ears and cozen her of all grace;
Enter upon the portion of her soul,
Her honour, which she calls her chastity,
And bring it into expense, for honesty
Is like a stock of money laid to sleep,
Which, ne'er so little broke, does never keep.
VINDICE. You have gi'n't the tang, i'faith, my lord.
Make known the lady to me and my brain

---

93 *waxed lines*: sealed letters.
99 *repugnant*: resisting.
112 *cozen*: cheat, trick.
113 *portion*: dowry.
115 *expense*: use.
118 *gi'n't the tang*: described it exactly.

Shall swell with strange invention: I will move it
Till I expire with speaking and drop down
Without a word to save me, but I'll work –

LUSSURIOSO. We thank thee and will raise thee; receive her name: it is the only daughter to madam Gratiana, the late widow.

VINDICE. (*aside*) O, my sister, my sister!

LUSSURIOSO. Why dost walk aside?

VINDICE. My lord, I was thinking how I might begin:
As thus, 'O lady' – or twenty hundred devices;
Her very bodkin will put a man in.

LUSSURIOSO. Ay, or the wagging of her hair.

VINDICE. No, that shall put you in, my lord.

LUSSURIORO. Shal't? Why, content. Dost know the daughter then?

VINDICE. O exc'lent well by sight.

LUSSURIOSO. That was her brother
That did prefer thee to us.

VINDICE. My lord, I think so;
I knew I had seen him somewhere.

LUSSURIOSO. And therefore, prithee, let thy heart to him
Be as a virgin, close.

VINDICE. O, my good lord.

LUSSURIOSO. We may laugh at that simple age within him . . .

VINDICE. Ha, ha, ha!

LUSSURIOSO. Himself being made the subtle instrument
To wind up a good fellow . . .

VINDICE. That's I, my lord.

LUSSURIOSO. That's thou . . .
To entice and work his sister.

VINDICE. A pure novice!

LUSSURIOSO. 'Twas finely managed.

VINDICE. Gallantly carried;
A pretty, perfumed villain.

LUSSURIOSO. I've bethought me,
If she prove chaste still and immovable,
Venture upon the mother and with gifts

---

129 *put a man in*: provide a chance to speak.

130–1 The sub-meaning is that Castiza's pubic hair will move to allow Lussurioso to enter her vagina.

141 *wind up*: incite.

As I will furnish thee begin with her.
VINDICE. O fie, fie! That's the wrong end, my lord. 'Tis mere impossible that a mother by any gifts should become a bawd to her own daughter!
LUSSURIOSO. Nay, then, I see thou'rt but a puny in the subtle mystery of a woman.
Why, 'tis held now no dainty dish: the name
Is so in league with age, that nowadays
It does eclipse three quarters of a mother.
VINDICE. Does't so, my lord?
Let me alone then to eclipse the fourth.
LUSSURIOSO. Why, well said; come I'll furnish thee, but first
Swear to be true in all.
VINDICE. True!
LUSSURIOSO. Nay, but swear!
VINDICE. Swear? I hope your honour little doubts my faith.
LUSSURIOSO. Yet for my humour's sake, 'cause I love swearing.
VINDICE. 'Cause you love swearing, 'slud, I will.
LUSSURIOSO. Why, enough.
Ere long look to be made of better stuff.
VINDICE. That will do well indeed, my lord.
LUSSURIOSO. Attend me!
Exit LUSSURIOSO.
VINDICE. O,
Now let me burst, I've eaten noble poison!
We are made strange fellows, brother, innocent villains.
Wilt not be angry when thou hear'st on't, think'st thou?
I'faith thou shalt. Swear me to foul my sister!
Sword, I durst make a promise of him to thee,
Thou shalt disheir him, it shall be thine honour.
And yet, now angry froth is down in me,
It would not prove the meanest policy
In this disguise to try the faith of both.
Another might have had the selfsame office,
Some slave that would have wrought effectually;

152 *puny*: puisnee; junior, beginner.
154 *name*: refers back to 'bawd' at l. 151.
163 *'slud*: By God's blood.

Ay, and perhaps o'erwrought 'em; therefore I,
Being thought travelled, will apply myself
Unto the selfsame form, forget my nature,
As if no part about me were kin to 'em;
So touch 'em – though I durst almost for good
Venture my lands in heaven upon their blood.

Exit VINDICE.

SCENE IV

Enter the discontented lord ANTONIO, *whose wife the duchess's* YOUNGEST SON *ravished; he discovering the body of her dead to certain lords,* PIERO *and* HIPPOLITO.

ANTONIO. Draw nearer, lords, and be sad witnesses
Of a fair, comely building newly fall'n,
Being falsely undermined: violent rape
Has played a glorious act. Behold, my lords,
A sight that strikes man out of me.
PIERO. That virtuous lady!
ANTONIO. Precedent for wives!
HIPPOLITO. The blush of many women, whose chaste presence
Would e'en call shame up to their cheeks
And make pale, wanton sinners have good colours.
ANTONIO. Dead!
Her honour first drunk poison, and her life,
Being fellows in one house, did pledge her honour.
PIERO. O grief of many!
ANTONIO. I marked not this before.
A prayer book the pillow to her cheek:
This was her rich confection and another
Placed in her right hand, with a leaf tucked up,
Pointing to these words:
'*Melius virtute mori, quam per dedecus vivere.*'
True and effectual it is indeed.

---

182 *touch*: test.
183 *blood*: see Textual note, p. 195.
6 *Precedent*: example.
15 *confection*: preservative (here obviously in the spiritual sense).
18 'Better to die virtuous than survive dishonour' (source unknown).

HIPPOLITO. My lord, since you invite us to your sorrows,
Let's truly taste 'em, that with equal comfort
As to ourselves we may relieve your wrongs.
We have grief too, that yet walks without tongue:
'*Curae leves loquuntur, majores stupent.*'
ANTONIO. You deal with truth, my lord.
Lend me but your attentions and I'll cut
Long grief into short words. Last revelling night,
When torchlight made an artificial noon
About the court, some courtiers in the masque,
Putting on better faces than their own,
Being full of fraud and flattery, amongst whom
The duchess' youngest son (that moth to honour)
Filled up a room; and with long lust to eat
Into my wearing, amongst all the ladies
Singled out that dear form, who ever lived
As cold in lust as she is now in death
(Which that step-duchess' monster knew too well)
And therefore in the height of all the revels,
When music was heard loudest, courtiers busiest,
And ladies great with laughter – O vicious minute!
Unfit but for relation to be spoke of –
Then with a face more impudent than his vizard
He harried her amidst a throng of pandars,
That live upon damnation of both kinds,
And fed the ravenous vulture of his lust.
O death to think on't! She, her honour forced,
Deemed it a nobler dowry for her name
To die with poison than to live with shame.
HIPPOLITO. A wondrous lady, of rare fire compact;
Sh'as made her name an empress by that act.
PIERO. My lord, what judgement follows the offender?
ANTONIO. Faith, none, my lord, it cools and is deferred.
PIERO. Delay the doom for rape!
ANTONIO. O, you must note who 'tis should die –
The duchess' son; she'll look to be a saver:
'Judgement in this age is near kin to favour.'

---

24 'Trifling cares are heard, greater ones are silent' (Seneca, *Hippolytus*,607, misquoted).
39 *heard*: see Textual note, p. 195.
43 *harried*: ravished.

HIPPOLITO. Nay, then, step forth thou bribeless officer.
He draws his sword.
I bind you all in steel to bind you surely:
Here let your oaths meet, to be kept and paid,
Which else will stick like rust and shame the blade;
Strengthen my vow, that if at the next sitting
Judgement speak all in gold, and spare the blood
Of such a serpent, e'en before their seats
To let his soul out, which long since was found
Guilty in heaven.
ALL. We swear it and will act it.
ANTONIO. Kind gentlemen, I thank you in mine ire.
HIPPOLITO. 'Twere pity
The ruins of so fair a monument
Should not be dipped in the defacer's blood.
PIERO. Her funeral shall be wealthy, for her name
Merits a tomb of pearl. My lord Antonio,
For this time wipe your lady from your eyes;
No doubt our grief and yours may one day court it
When we are more familiar with revenge.
ANTONIO. That is my comfort, gentlemen, and I joy
In this one happiness above the rest,
Which will be called a miracle at last,
That, being an old man, I'd a wife so chaste.
Exeunt all.

ACT II

SCENE I

Enter CASTIZA.

CASTIZA. How hardly shall that maiden be beset
Whose only fortunes are her constant thoughts,
That has no other child's part but her honour
That keeps her low and empty in estate.

76–7 Antonio is glancing at the traditional idea that for an old man to take a young wife is asking for trouble (Chaucer's 'Merchant's Tale' is a *locus classicus* of this theme).

1 *hardly*: severely.

3 *child's part*: inheritance.

Maids and their honours are like poor beginners;
Were not sin rich there would be fewer sinners.
Why had not virtue a revénue? Well,
I know the cause: 'twould have impoverished hell.

Enter DONDOLO.

How now, Dondolo?

DONDOLO. Madonna, there is one, as they say, a thing of flesh and blood, a man I take him by his beard, that would very desirously mouth to mouth with you.

CASTIZA. What's that?

DONDOLO. Show his teeth in your company.

CASTIZA. I understand thee not.

DONDOLO. Why, speak with you, madonna!

CASTISA. Why, say so, madman, and cut off a great deal of dirty way. Had it not been better spoke in ordinary words, that one would speak with me?

DONDOLO. Ha, ha, that's as ordinary as two shillings. I would strive a little to show myself in my place. A gentleman-usher scorns to use the phrase and fancy of a servingman.

CASTIZA. Yours be your own, sir. Go, direct him hither.

Exit DONDOLO.

I hope some happy tidings from my brother
That lately travelled, whom my soul affects.
Here he comes.

Enter VINDICE, *her brother, disguised.*

VINDICE. Lady, the best of wishes to your sex:
Fair skins and new gowns.

Gives her a letter.

CASTIZA. O, they shall thank you, sir.
Whence this?

VINDICE. O, from a dear and worthy friend,
Mighty!

CASTIZA. From whom?

VINDICE. The duke's son.

17–18 *cut . . . way*: i.e. speak directly ('avoid covering a lot of muddy ground').

26 *affects*: loves.

CASTIZA. Receive that!

A box o'th'ear to her brother.

I swore I'd put anger in my hand
And pass the virgin limits of my self
To him that next appeared in that base office,
To be his sin's attorney. Bear to him
The figure of my hate upon thy cheek
Whilst 'tis yet hot, and I'll reward thee for't;
Tell him my honour shall have a rich name
When several harlots shall share his with shame.
Farewell; commend me to him in my hate!

Exit CASTIZA.

VINDICE. It is the sweetest box that e'er my nose came nigh,
The finest drawn-work cuff that e'er was worn;
I'll love this blow forever, and this cheek
Shall still henceforward take the wall of this.
O, I'm above my tongue! Most constant sister,
In this thou hast right honourable shown;
Many are called by their honour that have none;
Thou art approved forever in my thoughts.
It is not in the power of words to taint thee,
And yet for the salvation of my oath,
As my resolve in that point I will lay
Hard siege unto my mother, though I know
A siren's tongue could not bewitch her so.
Mass, fitly here she comes!

Enter GRATIANA.

– Thanks my disguise. –
Madam, good afternoon.

GRATIANA. Y'are welcome, sir.

VINDICE. The next of Italy commends him to you,
Our mighty expectation, the duke's son.

---

36 *figure*: image.

41 Vindice plays on box = blow and = box of perfumed ointment.

42 *drawn-work cuff*: (a) cuff = blow; (b) cuff decorated with thread.

43–4 'This cheek will be privileged above the other' (Walking next to the wall was a privilege because the inner part of the pavement was cleaner).

53 *siren's tongue*: the sirens were mermaids who, in classical myth, drew sailors to death by their beautiful singing.

GRATIANA. I think myself much honoured that he pleases
To rank me in his thoughts.
VINDICE. So may you, lady:
One that is like to be our sudden duke;
The crown gapes for him every tide, and then
Commander o'er us all. Do but think on him;
How blessed were they now that could pleasure him,
E'en with anything almost.
GRATIANA. Ay, save their honour.
VINDICE. Tut, one would let a little of that go too
And ne'er be seen in't: ne'er be seen in't, mark you.
I'd wink and let it go.
GRATIANA. Marry, but I would not.
VINDICE. Marry, but I would I hope; I know you would too
If you'd that blood now which you gave your daughter.
To her indeed 'tis this wheel comes about;
That man that must be all this perhaps ere morning
(For his white father does but mould away)
Has long desired your daughter.
GRATIANA. Desired?
VINDICE. Nay, but hear me:
He desires now that will command hereafter;
Therefore be wise. I speak as more a friend
To you than him; madam, I know y'are poor,
And, lack the day,
There are too many poor ladies already.
Why should you vex the number? 'Tis despised.
Live wealthy, rightly understand the world
And chide away that foolish country girl
Keeps company with your daughter, Chastity.
GRATIANA. O fie, fie! The riches of the world cannot hire
A mother to such a most unnatural task.
VINDICE. No, but a thousand angels can:
Men have no power, angels must work you to't.
The world descends into such base-born evils

---

60 *sudden duke*: duke at any moment.
66 *in't*: see Textual note, p. 195.
72 *white*: pale, or white-haired.
80 *vex*: i.e. aggravate the condition of the poor ladies by adding to their number.
84–5 See Textual note, p. 195.
86–9 *angels*: used here (a) in the spiritual sense, (b) as = the English 10/– coin.

That forty angels can make fourscore devils.
There will be fools still, I perceive, still fools.
Would I be poor, dejected, scorned of greatness,
Swept from the palace and see other daughters
Spring with the dew o'th'court, having mine own
So much desired and loved – by the duke's son?
No, I would raise my state upon her breast
And call her eyes my tenants; I would count
My yearly maintenance upon her cheeks,
Take coach upon her lip, and all her parts
Should keep men after men and I would ride
In pleasure upon pleasure.
You took great pains for her, once when it was –
Let her requite it now, though it be but some.
You brought her forth; she may well bring you home.

GRATIANA. O heavens, this overcomes me!

VINDICE. (*aside*) Not, I hope, already?

GRATIANA. (*aside*) It is too strong for me; men know that know us
We are so weak their words can overthrow us.
He touched me nearly, made my virtues bate,
When his tongue struck upon my poor estate.

VINDICE. (*aside*) I e'en quake to proceed, my spirit turns edge,
I fear me she's unmothered, yet I'll venture:
'That woman is all male, whom none can enter.' –
What think you now, lady? Speak, are you wiser?
What said advancement to you? Thus it said:
'The daughter's fall lifts up the mother's head.'
Did it not, madam? But I'll swear it does
In many places; tut, this age fears no man.
' 'Tis no shame to be bad, because 'tis common.'

GRATIANA. Ay, that's the comfort on't.

VINDICE. The comfort on't!
I keep the best for last; can these persuade you
To forget heaven, and . . .

He gives her money.

GRATIANA. Ay, these are they . . .

---

90 *still fools*: see Textual note, p. 195.
103 *bring you home*: bring you to a position of financial security.
108 *bate*: abate, decline.
110 *turns edge*: grows blunt.

VINDICE. O!
GRATIANA. . . . that enchant our sex, these are the means
That govern our affections: that woman
Will not be troubled with the mother long
That sees the comfortable shine of you:
I blush to think what for your sakes I'll do!
VINDICE. (*aside*) O suff'ring heaven, with thy invisible
finger
E'en at this instant turn the precious side
Of both mine eyeballs inward, not to see myself.
GRATIANA. Look you, sir.
VINDICE. Holla.
GRATIANA. Let this thank your pains.
She gives him money.
VINDICE. O, you're a kind madam.
GRATIANA. I'll see how I can move.
VINDICE. Your words will sting.
GRATIANA. If she be still chaste I'll ne'er call her mine.
VINDICE. (*aside*) Spoke truer than you meant it.
GRATIANA. Daughter Castiza.

Enter CASTIZA.

CASTIZA. Madam.
VINDICE. O, she's yonder;
Meet her.
(*Aside*) Troops of celestial soldiers guard her heart:
Yon dam has devils enough to take her part.
CASTIZA. Madam, what makes yon evil-officed man
In presence of you?
GRATIANA. Why?
CASTIZA. He lately brought
Immodest writing sent from the duke's son
To tempt me to dishonourable act.
GRATIANA. Dishonourable act? Good honourable fool,
That wouldst be honest 'cause thou wouldst be so,
Producing no one reason but thy will –
And 'tas a good report, prettily commended,
But, pray, by whom? Mean people, ignorant people;
The better sort, I'm sure, cannot abide it –

---

124 *troubled . . . mother*: Will not be long disturbed by conscience.
131 *kind*: with sub-meaning 'natural'.
madam: see Textual note, p. 195.

And by what rule should we square out our lives
But by our betters' actions? O, if thou knew'st
What 'twere to lose it thou would never keep it.
But there's a cold curse laid upon all maids,
Whilst others clip the sun, they clasp the shades.
Virginity is paradise locked up:
You cannot come by yourselves without fee,
And 'twas decreed that man should keep the key.
Deny advancement, treasure, the duke's son?
CASTIZA. I cry you mercy, lady, I mistook you.
Pray, did you see my mother? Which way went you?
Pray God I have not lost her.
VINDICE. (*aside*) Prettily put by.
GRATIANA. Are you as proud to me as coy to him?
Do you not know me now?
CASTIZA. Why, are you she?
The world's so changed, one shape into another,
It is a wise child now that knows her mother.
VINDICE. (*aside*) Most right, i'faith.
GRATIANA. I owe your cheek my hand.
Come, you shall leave those childish 'haviours
And understand your time. Fortunes flow to you;
What, will you be a girl?
If all feared drowning that spy waves ashore,
Gold would grow rich and all the merchants poor.
CASTIZA. It is a pretty saying of a wicked one;
But methinks now
It does show so well out of your mouth:
Better in his.
VINDICE. (*aside*) Faith, bad enough in both,
Were I in earnest, as I'll seem no less. –
I wonder, lady, your own mother's words
Cannot be taken, nor stand in full force.
'Tis honesty you urge: what's honesty?
'Tis but heaven's beggar,
And what woman is so foolish to keep honesty
And not be able to keep herself? No,

---

149 *should*: see Textual note, p. 195.
square out: organise, shape.
153 *others*: see Textual note, p. 195.
clip: embrace.
155 *fee*: payment.
156 *key*: with sub-meaning 'penis'.

Times are grown wiser and will keep less charge.
A maid that has small portion now intends
To break up house and live upon her friends.
How blessed are you. You have happiness alone;
Others must fall to thousands, you to one,
Sufficient in himself to make your forehead
Dazzle the world with jewels, and petitionary people
Start at your presence.

GRATIANA. O, if I were young
I should be ravished.

CASTIZA. Ay, to lose your honour.

VINDICE. 'Slid, how can you lose your honour
To deal with my lord's grace?
He'll add more honour to it by his title:
Your mother will tell you how.

GRATIANA. That I will.

VINDICE. O, think upon the pleasure of the palace:
Securèd ease and state; the stirring meats
Ready to move out of the dishes,
That e'en now quicken when they're eaten;
Banquets abroad by torchlight, musics, sports,
Bareheaded vassals that had ne'er the fortune
To keep on their own hats, but let horns wear 'em;
Nine coaches waiting, hurry, hurry, hurry!

CASTIZA. Ay, to the devil.

VINDICE. (*aside*) Ay, to the devil. – To th'duke, by my faith.

GRATIANA. Ay, to the duke, daughter: you'd scorn to think
O'th'devil an you were there once.

VINDICE. (*aside*) True, for most
There are as proud as he for his heart, i'faith. –
Who'd sit at home in a neglected room
Dealing her short-lived beauty to the pictures,

---

182 *charge*: expense; also 'care less about virtue'.
183 *portion*: dowry, marriage portion.
188 *petitionary people*: people with suits or petitions to present to others in great positions.
191 *'Slid*: By God's eyelid.
196 *Securèd*: certain, stable.
stirring: stimulating.
198 *quicken*: come to life.
205–7 See Textual note, p. 195.

That are as useless as old men, when those
Poorer in face and fortune than herself
Walk with a hundred acres on their backs,
Fair meadows cut into green foreparts? O,
It was the greatest blessing ever happened to woman
When farmers' sons agreed and met again
To wash their hands and come up gentlemen.
The commonwealth has flourished ever since:
Lands that were mete by the rod, that labour's spared;
Tailors ride down and measure 'em by the yard.
Fair trees, those comely foretops of the field,
Are cut to maintain head-tires – much untold.
All thrives but Chastity – she lies a-cold.
Nay, shall I come nearer to you? Mark but this:
Why are there so few honest women but because 'tis the poorer profession? That's accounted best that's best followed; least in trade, least in fashion; and that's not honesty, believe it.
And do but note the love and dejected price of it:
Lose but a pearl, we search and cannot brook it;
But that once gone, who is so mad to look it?

GRATIANA. Troth, he says true.

CASTIZA. False! I defy you both.
I have endured you with an ear of fire;
Your tongues have struck hot irons on my face:
Mother, come from that poisonous woman there.

GRATIANA. Where?

CASTIZA. Do you not see her? She's too inward then. –
Slave, perish in thy office! – You heavens, please
Henceforth to make the mother a disease
Which first begins with me; yet I've outgone you.

Exit CASTIZA.

VINDICE. (*aside*) O angels, clap your wings upon the skies

---

213 *foreparts*: 'ornamental coverings for the breast' (Foakes).
216f. *come up gentlemen*: rise in social position (ll. 216ff. refer satirically to contemporary social movements).
218 *mete*: measured.
220 *foretops*: forelocks.
221 *head-tires*: headdresses.
228 *love*: see Textual note, p. 195.
229 *brook it*: endure its loss.

And give this virgin crystal plaudities!
GRATIANA. Peevish, coy, foolish! But return this answer:
My lord shall be most welcome when his pleasure
Conducts him this way. I will sway mine own:
Women with women can work best alone.
Exit GRATIANA.
VINDICE. Indeed, I'll tell him so.
O, more uncivil, more unnatural
Than those base-titled creatures that look downward,
Why does not heaven turn black or with a frown
Undo the world? Why does not earth start up
And strike the sins that tread upon't? O,
Were't not for gold and women there would be no damnation:
Hell would look like a lord's great kitchen without fire in't:
But 'twas decreed before the world began
That they should be the hooks to catch at man.
Exit VINDICE.

SCENE II

Enter LUSSURIOSO *with* HIPPOLITO.

LUSSURIOSO. I much applaud thy judgement:
Thou art well read in a fellow,
And 'tis the deepest art to study man.
I know this, which I never learnt in schools,
The world's divided into knaves and fools.
HIPPOLITO. (*aside*) Knave in your face, my lord – behind your back.
LUSSURIOSO. And I much thank thee that thou hast preferred
A fellow of discourse, well mingled,
And whose brain time hath seasoned.
HIPPOLITO. True, my lord.
(*Aside*) We shall find season once, I hope. O villain!
To make such an unnatural slave of me; but . . .

---

240 *plaudities*: applause.
247 Man was distinguished from the brute beasts by walking upright.
7 *preferred*: recommended.
8 *discourse*: fluent conversation.
10 *season*: i.e. the right time for revenge.

Mass, here he comes.

Enter VINDICE *disguised.*

(*Aside*) And now shall I have free leave to depart.
LUSSURIOSO. Your absence, leave us.
HIPPOLITO. Are not my thoughts true?
(*To Vindice*) I must remove, but, brother, you may stay:
Heart, we are both made bawds a new-found way!

Exit HIPPOLITO.

LUSSURIOSO. Now we're an even number; a third man's
Dangerous; especially her brother; say, be free,
Have I a pleasure toward?
VINDICE. O my lord!
LUSSURIOSO. Ravish me in thine answer; art thou rare?
Hast thou beguiled her with honey? Is she a woman?
VINDICE. In all but in desire.
LUSSURIOSO. Then she's in nothing –
I bate in courage now.
VINDICE. The words I brought
Might well have made indifferent honest naught.
A right good woman in these days is changed
Into white money with less labour far;
Many a maid has turned to Mahomet
With easier working. I durst undertake,
Upon the pawn and forfeit of my life,
With half those words to flat a Puritan's wife,
But she is close and good; yet 'tis a doubt
By this time. O, the mother, the mother!
LUSSURIOSO. I never thought their sex had been a wonder
Until this minute: what fruit from the mother?
VINDICE. (*aside*) Now must I blister my soul, be forsworn,
Or shame the woman that received me first.
I will be true; thou liv'st not to proclaim:
Spoke to a dying man shame has no shame. –
My lord.

---

19 *toward*: imminent.
20 *rare*: of great value (through succeeding in your task).
23 *bate*: abate, lose.
26 *white money*: silver.
27 i.e. has become a pagan in morals as well as in religion.
30 *flat*: (a) overcome in debate; (b) put her on her back.
31–2 See Textual note, p. 195.

LUSSURIOSO. Who's that?
VINDICE. Here's none but I, my lord.
LUSSURIOSO. What would thy haste utter?
VINDICE. Comfort.
LUSSURIOSO. Welcome.
VINDICE. The maid being dull, having no mind to travel
Into unknown lands, what did me straight,
But set spurs to the mother? Golden spurs
Will put her to a false gallop in a trice.
LUSSURIOSO. Is't possible that in this
The mother should be damned before the daughter?
VINDICE. O, that's good manners, my lord: the mother for her age must go foremost, you know.
LUSSURIOSO. Thou spok'st that true, but where comes in this comfort?
VINDICE. In a fine place, my lord. The unnatural mother
Did with her tongue so hard beset her honour
That the poor fool was struck to silent wonder;
Yet still the maid, like an unlighted taper,
Was cold and chaste, save that her mother's breath
Did blow fire on her cheeks. The girl departed
But the good ancient madam, half-mad, threw me
These promising words, which I took deeply note of:
'My lord shall be most welcome . . .'
LUSSURIOSO. Faith, I thank her.
VINDICE. ' . . . when his pleasure conducts him this way . . .'
LUSSURIOSO. That shall be soon, i'faith.
VINDICE. ' . . . I will sway mine own . . .'
LUSSURIOSO. She does the wiser; I commend her for't.
VINDICE. ' . . . Women with women can work best alone.'
LUSSURIOSO. By this light, and so they can, give 'em their due, men are not comparable to 'em.
VINDICE. No, that's true, for you shall have one woman knit more in an hour than any man can ravel again in seven and twenty year.
LUSSURIOSO. Now my desires are happy; I'll make 'em freemen now.
Thou art a precious fellow; faith, I love thee;
Be wise and make it thy revénue: beg, leg!

---

55 *cheeks*: see Textual note, p. 195.
66 *ravel*: unravel.
70 *leg*: bow.

What office couldst thou be ambitious for?

VINDICE. Office, my lord? Marry, if I might have my wish, I would have one that was never begged yet.

LUSSURIOSO. Nay, then thou canst have none.

VINDICE. Yes, my lord, I could pick out another office yet; nay, and keep a horse and drab upon't.

LUSSURIOSO. Prithee, good bluntness, tell me.

VINDICE. Why, I would desire but this, my lord: to have all the fees behind the arras, and all the farthingales that fall plump about twelve o'clock at night upon the rushes.

LUSSURIOSO. Thou'rt a mad, apprehensive knave. Dost think to make any great purchase of that?

VINDICE. O, 'tis an unknown thing, my lord; I wonder 'tas been missed so long.

LUSSURIOSO. Well, this night I'll visit her, and 'tis till then
A year in my desires. Farewell – Attend! –
Trust me with thy preferment. *Exit* LUSSURIOSO.

VINDICE. My loved lord.
O shall I kill him o'th'wrong side now? No!
Sword, thou wast never a backbiter yet.
I'll pierce him to his face; he shall die looking upon me.
Thy veins are swelled with lust; this shall unfill 'em:
Great men were gods if beggars could not kill 'em.
Forgive me, heaven, to call my mother wicked;
O lessen not my days upon the earth.
I cannot honour her. By this, I fear me,
Her tongue has turned my sister into use.
I was a villain not to be forsworn
To this our lecherous hope, the duke's son,
For lawyers, merchants, some divines and all,

71f. These lines allude satirically to Jacobean abuse in the distribution of monopolies – some grants were for things scarcely less bizarre than those that Vindice here asks for.

76 *drab*: whore.

79 *farthingales*: hooped petticoats.

82 *apprehensive*: witty.

83 *purchase*: profit.

89 *o'th'wrong side*: in the back.

94–5 Echoing *Exodus* 20:12.

96 *by this*: by this time.

97 *into use*: into a potential whore.

Count beneficial perjury a sin small.
It shall go hard yet but I'll guard her honour
And keep the ports sure.

Enter HIPPOLITO.

HIPPOLITO. Brother, how goes the world?
I would know news of you, but I have news
To tell you.
VINDICE. What, in the name of knavery?
HIPPOLITO. Knavery, faith:
The vicious old duke's worthily abused;
The pen of his bastard writes him cuckold!
VINDICE. His bastard?
HIPPOLITO. Pray believe it: he and the duchess
By night meet in their linen; they have been seen
By stair-foot panders.
VINDICE. O sin foul and deep!
Great faults are winked at when the duke's asleep.
See, see, here comes the Spurio.
HIPPOLITO. Monstrous luxur!

Enter SPURIO *with two servants.*

VINDICE. Unbraced; two of his valiant bawds with him.
O, there's a wicked whisper; hell is in his ear.
Stay, let's observe his passage.
They withdraw.
SPURIO. O, but are you sure on't?
SERVANT. My lord, most sure on't, for 'twas spoke by one
That is most inward with the duke's son's lust,

---

101 *beneficial perjury*: acceptable lying for a good purpose.
103 *ports*: gates.
108 *pen*: with the sexual meaning 'penis'. (In the notorious Essex/Howard divorce case the Lord Chamberlain remarked 'that it was truth that the earl had no ink in his pen: that . . . he could not know a woman' – quoted from B. White *Cast of Ravens* (John Murray, 1965), p. 42, and cf. p. 44.)
113 *luxur*: lecher.
114 *Unbraced*: with clothes unfastened.
116 It is important for the development of the plot to note that Vindice and Hippolito do not hear what Spurio and the servant discuss: Vindice makes a false inference as to what Spurio is about to do.

That he intends within this hour to steal
Unto Hippolito's sister, whose chaste life
The mother has corrupted for his use.

SPURIO. Sweet word, sweet occasion! Faith then brother,
I'll disinherit you in as short time
As I was when I was begot in haste;
I'll damn you at your pleasure: precious deed!
After your lust, O, 'twill be fine to bleed.
Come, let our passing out be soft and wary.

Exeunt SPURIO *and servants.*

VINDICE. Mark, there, there, that step! Now to the duchess.
This their second meeting writes the duke cuckold
With new additions, his horns newly revived.
Night! Thou that look'st like funeral herald's fees
Torn down betimes i'th'morning, thou hang'st fitly
To grace those sins that have no grace at all.
Now 'tis full sea abed over the world,
There's juggling of all sides: some that were maids
E'en at sunset are now perhaps i'th'toll-book;
This woman in immodest thin apparel
Lets in her friend by water; here a dame
Cunning nails leather hinges to a door
To avoid proclamation; now cuckolds are
A-coining, apace, apace, apace, apace!
And careful sisters spin that thread i'th'night
That does maintain them and their bawds i'th'day!

HIPPOLITO. You flow well, brother.

VINDICE. Pooh, I'm shallow yet,
Too sparing and too modest. Shall I tell thee?
If every trick were told that's dealt by night
There are few here that would not blush outright.

---

132 *fees*: 'for phease or pheese, which means tatters or hangings . . . In this place then it would mean the black frieze put up on the occasion of a funeral, which remaining for the night was taken down next morning' (Collins).

137 *toll-book*: a book recording the sale of animals: here obviously a register of prostitutes.

141 *To avoid proclamation*: to avoid having her sin discovered.

143 *sisters*: prostitutes.

147 *trick*: card hand/device/sexual bout.
told: revealed/counted.
dealt: dealing of cards/playing of sexual games.

148–50 See Textual note, p. 195.

HIPPOLITO. I am of that belief too.
VINDICE. Who's this comes?

Enter LUSSURIOSO.

The duke's son up so late? Brother, fall back
And you shall learn some mischief.

HIPPOLITO *withdraws.*

My good lord.
LUSSURIOSO. Piato! Why, the man I wished for! Come,
I do embrace this season for the fittest
To taste of that young lady.
VINDICE. (*aside*) Heart and hell.
HIPPOLITO. (*aside*) Damned villain.
VINDICE. (*aside*) I ha' no way now to cross it
But to kill him.
LUSSURIOSO. Come, only thou and I.
VINDICE. My lord, my lord!
LUSSURIOSO. Why dost thou start us?
VINDICE. I'd almost forgot – the bastard!
LUSSURIOSO. What of him?
VINDICE. This night, this hour, this minute, now . . .
LUSSURIOSO. What, what?
VINDICE. Shadows the duchess . . .
LUSSURIOSO. Horrible word.
VINDICE. And like strong poison eats
Into the duke your father's forehead.
LUSSURIOSO. O!
VINDICE. He makes horn royal.
LUSSURIOSO. Most ignoble slave!
VINDICE. This is the fruit of two beds.
LUSSURIOSO. I am mad.
VINDICE. That passage he trod warily . . .
LUSSURIOSO. He did?
VINDICE. And hushed his villains every step he took.
LUSSURIOSO. His villains? I'll confound them.
VINDICE. Take 'em finely, finely now.
LUSSURIOSO. The duchess' chamber door shall not control me.

---

152 *Piato*: Vindice's assumed name means 'hidden'.
157 *start*: startle.
160 *Shadows*: covers sexually.

Exeunt LUSSURIOSO *and* VINDICE.

HIPPOLITO. Good, happy, swift, there's gunpowder i'th'court,
Wildfire at midnight! In this heedless fury
He may show violence to cross himself.
I'll follow the event. *Exit* HIPPOLITO.

SCENE III

The DUKE *and* DUCHESS *in bed. Enter* LUSSURIOSO *and* VINDICE *disguised.*

LUSSURIOSO. Where is that villain?
VINDICE. Softly, my lord, and you may take 'em twisted.
LUSSURIOSO. I care not how!
VINDICE. O, 'twill be glorious
To kill 'em doubled, when they're heaped. Be soft, my lord.
LUSSURIOSO. Away, my spleen is not so lazy; thus and thus
I'll shake their eyelids ope, and with my sword
Shut 'em again forever. – Villain! Strumpet!
DUKE. You upper guard, defend us!
DUCHESS. Treason, treason!
DUKE. O take me not in sleep!
I have great sins, I must have days,
Nay months, dear son, with penitential heaves,
To lift 'em out and not to die unclear.
O, thou wilt kill me both in heaven and here.
LUSSURIOSO. I am amazed to death.
DUKE. Nay, villain, traitor,
Worse than the foulest epithet, now I'll gripe thee
E'en with the nerves of wrath, and throw thy head
Amongst the lawyers! – Guard!

Enter nobles, AMBITIOSO *and* SUPERVACUO, HIPPOLITO.

---

171 *Wildfire*: combustible material used for starting fires.
172 *cross*: foil.
2 *twisted*: in coition.
8 *upper guard*: the guard nearest the bedchamber.
11 *heaves*: sighs.
15 *gripe*: see Textual note, p. 195.

FIRST NOBLE. How comes the quiet of your grace
disturbed?
DUKE. This boy, that should be myself after me,
Would be myself before me, and in heat
Of that ambition bloodily rushed in,
Intending to depose me in my bed!
SECOND NOBLE. Duty and natural loyalty forfend!
DUCHESS. He called his father villain and me strumpet,
A word that I abhor to 'file my lips with.
AMBITIOSO. That was not so well done, brother.
LUSSURIOSO. (*aside*) I am abused,
I know there is no excuse can do me good.
VINDICE. (*to Hippolito*) 'Tis now good policy to be from
sight:
His vicious purpose to our sister's honour
Is crossed beyond our thought.
HIPPOLITO. You little dreamt
His father slept here?
VINDICE. O, 'twas far beyond me.
But since it fell so, without frightful word,
Would he had killed him: 'twould have eased our
swords. *Exeunt* VINDICE *and* HIPPOLITO.
DUKE. Be comforted, our duchess, he shall die.
LUSSURIOSO. (*aside*) Where's this slave-pandar now?
Out of mine eye,
Guilty of this abuse.

Enter SPURIO *with his villains.*

SPURIO. Y'are villains, fablers!
You have knaves' chins and harlots' tongues; you lie,
And I will damn you with one meal a day.
FIRST SERVANT. O good my lord!
SPURIO. 'Sblood, you shall
never sup.
SECOND SERVANT. O, I beseech you, sir!
SPURIO. To let my sword
Catch cold so long, and miss him.
FIRST SERVANT. Troth, my lord,
'Twas his intent to meet there.

---

25 *'file*: defile.
27 *abused*: misled.
34 s.d. See Textual note, p. 195.

SPURIO. Heart, he's yonder.
Ha, what news here? Is the day out o'th'socket
That it is noon at midnight? The court up?
How comes the guard so saucy with his elbows?
LUSSURIOSO. (*aside*) The bastard here?
Nay, then the truth of my intent shall out.
My lord and father, hear me.
DUKE. Bear him hence.
LUSSURIOSO. I can with loyalty excuse . . .
DUKE. Excuse? To prison with the villain!
Death shall not long lag after him.
SPURIO. (*aside*) Good, i'faith, then 'tis not much amiss.
LUSSURIOSO. Brothers, my best release lies on your tongues;
I pray, persuade for me.
AMBITIOSO. It is our duties; make yourself sure of us.
SUPERVACUO. We'll sweat in pleading.
LUSSURIOSO. And I may live to thank you.
Exeunt LUSSURIOSO *and guards.*
AMBITIOSO. (*aside*) No, thy death shall thank me better.
SPURIO. (*aside*) He's gone; I'll after him
And know his trespass, seem to bear a part
In all his ills, but with a Puritan heart.
Exit SPURIO *with his villains.*
AMBITIOSO. (*to Supervacuo*) Now, brother, let our hate and love be woven
So subtly together that in speaking
One word for his life we may make three for his death.
The craftiest pleader gets most gold for breath.
SUPERVACUO. Set on – I'll not be far behind you, brother.
DUKE. Is't possible a son should be disobedient as far as the sword?
It is the highest; he can go no farther.
AMBITIOSO. My gracious lord, take pity.
DUKE. Pity, boys?
AMBITIOSO. Nay, we'd be loath to move your grace too much;
We know the trespass is unpardonable,
Black, wicked and unnatural.
SUPERVACUO. In a son, O monstrous!

---

44 *socket*: normal position.
61 *Puritan*: hypocritical.

AMBITIOSO. Yet, my lord,
A duke's soft hand strokes the rough head of law
And makes it lie smooth.
DUKE. But my hand shall ne'er do't.
AMBITIOSO. That as you please, my lord.
SUPERVACUO. We must needs confess
Some father would have entered into hate
So deadly pointed that before his eyes
He would ha'seen the execution sound
Without corrupted favour.
AMBITIOSO. But, my lord,
Your grace may live the wonder of all times,
In pardoning that offence which never yet
Had face to beg a pardon.
DUKE. Honey, how's this?
AMBITIOSO. Forgive him, good my lord: he's your own son,
And I must say 'twas the vildlier done.
SUPERVACUO. He's the next heir; yet this true reason gathers,
None can possess that dispossess their fathers.
Be merciful.
DUKE. (*aside*) Here's no stepmother's wit;
I'll try 'em both upon their love and hate.
AMBITIOSO. Be merciful, although . . .
DUKE. You have prevailed.
My wrath, like flaming wax, hath spent itself.
I know 'twas but some peevish moon in him;
Go, let him be released.
SUPERVACUO. (*to Ambitioso*) 'Sfoot, how now brother?
AMBITIOSO. Your grace doth please to speak beside your spleen;
I would it were so happy.
DUKE. Why, go release him.
SUPERVACUO. O, my good lord, I know the fault's too weighty

---

79 *sound*: fully carried out.
85 *vildlier*: more vilely.
88 This seems to mean that the duke thinks that Supervacuo and Ambitioso lack the intelligence of their stepmother, since they have not managed to deceive him.
92 *peevish moon*: fit induced by the moon.
94 *beside your spleen*: putting your anger aside.

And full of general loathing, too inhumane,
Rather by all men's voices worthy death.
DUKE. 'Tis true too.
Here, then, receive this signet: doom shall pass.
Direct it to the judges; he shall die
Ere many days. Make haste.
AMBITIOSO. All speed that may be.
We could have wished his burden not so sore;
We know your grace did but delay before.
Exeunt AMBITIOSO *and* SUPERVACUO.
DUKE. Here's envy with a poor thin cover o'er't,
Like scarlet hid in lawn, easily spied through.
This their ambition by the mother's side
Is dangerous and for safety must be purged.
I will prevent their envies; sure it was
But some mistaken fury in our son,
Which these aspiring boys would climb upon:
He shall be released suddenly.

Enter nobles.

FIRST NOBLE. Good morning to your grace.
DUKE. Welcome, my lords.
SECOND NOBLE. Our knees shall take away
The office of our feet forever,
Unless your grace bestow a father's eye
Upon the clouded fortunes of your son,
And in compassionate virtue grant him that
Which makes e'en mean men happy – liberty.
DUKE. (*aside*) How seriously their loves and honours woo
For that which I am about to pray them do. –
Which (rise my lords) your knees sign: his release.
We freely pardon him.
FIRST NOBLE. We owe your grace much thanks, and he much duty.
Exeunt nobles.
DUKE. It well becomes that judge to nod at crimes,
That does commit greater himself and lives.
I may forgive a disobedient error

---

106 *lawn*: thin, fine linen.
109 *prevent*: forestall.
112 *suddenly*: quickly.
122 See Textual note, p. 195.

That expect pardon for adultery,
And in my old days am a youth in lust.
Many a beauty have I turned to poison
In the denial, covetous of all.
Age hot is like a monster to be seen:
My hairs are white and yet my sins are green.
Exit DUKE.

ACT III

SCENE I

Enter AMBITIOSO *and* SUPERVACUO.

SUPERVACUO. Brother, let my opinion sway you once.
I speak it for the best, to have him die
Surest and soonest. If the signet come
Unto the judges' hands, why then his doom
Will be deferred till sittings and court days,
Juries and further. Faiths are bought and sold:
Oaths in these days are but the skin of gold.
AMBITIOSO. In troth, 'tis true too.
SUPERVACUO. Then let's set by the judges
And fall to the officers. 'Tis but mistaking
The duke our father's meaning, and where he named
'Ere many days', 'tis but forgetting that
And have him die i'th'morning.
AMBITIOSO. Excellent!
Then am I heir – duke in a minute!
SUPERVACUO. (*aside*) Nay,
And he were once puffed out, here is a pin
Should quickly prick your bladder.
AMBITIOSO. Blessed occasion!

---

131 *in the denial*: because she denied me what I wanted.
133 *green*: youthful.
7 *Oaths . . . gold*: Nowadays oaths serve merely as cover for the real force – money.
8 *set by*: ignore.
9 *fall to*: concentrate on.
14 *pin*: sword.
15 *Blessed*: see Textual note, p. 195.

He being packed we'll have some trick and wile
To wind our younger brother out of prison
That lies in for the rape. The lady's dead
And people's thoughts will soon be burièd.

SUPERVACUO. We may with safety do't, and live and feed:
The duchess' sons are too proud to bleed.

AMBITIOSO. We are, i'faith, to say true. Come, let's not linger.
I'll to the officers; go you before
And set an edge upon the executioner.

SUPERVACUO. Let me along to grind him.

Exit SUPERVACUO.

AMBITIOSO. Meet, farewell.
I am next now; I rise just in that place
Where thou'rt cut off, upon thy neck, kind brother:
The falling of one head lifts up another.

SCENE II

Enter with the nobles LUSSURIOSO *from prison.*

LUSSURIOSO. My lords, I am much indebted to your loves
For this, O this delivery.

FIRST NOBLE. But our duties,
My lord, unto the hopes that grow in you.

LUSSURIOSO. If e'er I live to be myself I'll thank you.
O liberty, thou sweet and heavenly dame!
But hell for prison is too mild a name!

Exeunt LUSSURIOSO *and nobles.*

SCENE III

Enter AMBITIOSO *and* SUPERVACUO *with officers.*

AMBITIOSO. Officers, here's the duke's signet, your firm warrant,
Brings the command of present death along with it
Unto our brother, the duke's son. We are sorry

---

16 *packed*: dispatched.
25 *Meet*: Just right!
2 *But*: only
2 *present*: immediate.

That we are so unnaturally employed
In such an unkind office, fitter far
For enemies than brothers.

SUPERVACUO. But you know
The duke's command must be obeyed.

FIRST OFFICER. It must and shall, my lord. This morning then;
So suddenly?

AMBITIOSO. Ay, alas! Poor, good soul,
He must breakfast betimes; the executioner
Stands ready to put forth his cowardly valour.

SECOND OFFICER. Already?

SUPERVACUO. Already, i'faith. O, sir, destruction hies,
And that is least impúdent, soonest dies.

FIRST OFFICER. Troth, you say true, my lord; we take our leaves.
Our office shall be sound; we'll not delay
The third part of a minute.

AMBITIOSO. Therein you show
Yourselves good men and upright officers.
Pray, let him die as private as he may;
Do him that favour, for the gaping people
Will but trouble him at his prayers
And make him curse and swear and so die black.
Will you be so far kind?

FIRST OFFICER. It shall be done, my lord.

AMBITIOSO. Why, we do thank you; if we live to be,
You shall have a better office.

SECOND OFFICER. Your good lordship.

SUPERVACUO. Commend us to the scaffold in our tears.

FIRST OFFICER. We'll weep and do your commendations.

Exeunt officers.

AMBITIOSO. Fine fools in office!

SUPERVACUO. Things fall out so fit!

AMBITIOSO. So happily! Come, brother, ere next clock
His head will be made to serve a bigger block.

---

5 *unkind*: 'unnatural' as well as 'cruel'.
13 *hies*: draws near.
14 *impúdent*: see Textual note, p. 195.
16 *sound*: see Textual note, p. 195.
22 *black*: i.e. damned.
30 *block*: his head will soon fit the headsman's block, which is larger than his hats were ('block' can mean 'hat size').

SCENE IV

Enter, in prison, the YOUNGEST SON *and his sister.*

YOUNGEST SON. Keeper.
KEEPER. My lord?
YOUNGEST SON. No news lately from our brothers?
Are they unmindful of us?
KEEPER. My lord, a messenger came newly in
And brought this from 'em.
Gives him a letter.
YOUNGEST SON. Nothing but paper comforts?
I looked for my delivery before this
Had they been worth their oaths. Prithee, be from us.
Exit keeper.
Now, what say you, forsooth? Speak out, I pray.
(*Reads the letter*) 'Brother, be of good cheer':
'Slud, it begins like a whore with good cheer.
'Thou shalt not be long a prisoner.'
Not five and thirty, like a bankrout –
I think so.
'We have thought upon a device to get thee out by a trick.'
By a trick!
Pox o'your trick and it be so long a-playing.
'And so rest comforted, be merry and expect it suddenly.'
Be merry! Hang merry, draw and quarter merry!
I'll be mad. (*Tears up the letter*) Is't not strange that a man should lie in a whole month for a woman? Well, we shall see how sudden our brothers will be in their promise.
I must expect still a trick: I shall not be long a prisoner.

Enter keeper.

How now, what news?

---

9 *'Slud*: By God's blood.
11 *bankrout*: bankrupt.
18–19 *strange . . . woman'*: as well as the obvious meaning there is a paradoxical one – 'Isn't it odd that a man should be confined for a month because of a woman: the natural thing is for the woman to be confined in childbed because a man has impregnated her.'
22 See Textual note, p. 195.

KEEPER. Bad news, my lord, I am discharged of you.
YOUNGEST SON. Slave, call'st thou that bad news? – I thank you brothers.
KEEPER. My lord, 'twill prove so; here come the officers
Into whose hands I must commit you.

Enter officers.

YOUNGEST SON. Ha?
Officers? What? Why?
FIRST OFFICER. You must pardon us, my lord,
Our office must be sound. Here is our warrant,
The signet from the duke: you must straight suffer.
YOUNGEST SON. Suffer? I'll suffer you to be gone; I'll suffer you
To come no more. What would you have me suffer?
SECOND OFFICER. My lord, those words were better changed to prayers,
The time's but brief with you; prepare to die.
YOUNGEST SON. Sure 'tis not so.
THIRD OFFICER. It is too true, my lord.
YOUNGEST SON. I tell you 'tis not, for the duke my father
Deferred me till next sitting and I look
E'en every minute, threescore times an hour,
For a release, a trick wrought by my brothers.
FIRST OFFICER. A trick, my lord? If you expect such comfort
Your hope's as fruitless as a barren woman:
Your brothers were the unhappy messengers
That brought this powerful token for your death.
YOUNGEST SON. My brothers? No, no.
SECOND OFFICER. 'Tis most true, my lord.
YOUNGEST SON. My brothers to bring a warrant for my death?
How strange this shows!
THIRD OFFICER. There's no delaying time.
YOUNGEST SON. Desire 'em hither, call 'em up, my brothers!
They shall deny it to your faces.
FIRST OFFICER. My lord,
They're far enough by this, at least at court,
And this most strict command they left behind 'em

29 *sound*: thoroughly performed.

When grief swum in their eyes: they showed like brothers,
Brimful of heavy sorrow, but the duke
Must have his pleasure.
YOUNGEST SON. His pleasure!
FIRST OFFICER. These were their last words which my memory bears:
'Commend us to the scaffold in our tears.'
YOUNGEST SON. Pox dry their tears! What should I do with tears?
I hate 'em worse than any citizen's son
Can hate salt water. Here came a letter now,
New-bleeding from their pens, scarce stinted yet –
Would I'd been torn to pieces when I tore it.
Tries to piece the letter together.
Look you officious whoresons, words of comfort:
'Not long a prisoner'.
FIRST OFFICER. It says true in that, sir, for you must suffer presently.
YOUNGEST SON. A villainous Duns upon the letter – knavish exposition.
Look you then here, sir: 'We'll get thee out by a trick', says he.
SECOND OFFICER. That may hold too, sir, for you know a trick is commonly four cards, which was meant by us four officers.
YOUNGEST SON. Worse and worse dealing.
FIRST OFFICER. The hour beckons us,
The headsman waits; lift up your eyes to heaven.
YOUNGEST SON. I thank you, faith; good, pretty-wholesome counsel!
I should look up to heaven, as you said,
Whilst he behind me cozens me of my head.
Ay, that's the trick.
THIRD OFFICER. You delay too long, my lord.

57–8 Foakes quotes the proverb 'Praise the sea but keep on land.'
59 *stinted*: staunched.
64 *Duns upon the letter*: i.e. 'to hell with your literal quibbling on the letter's meaning'. Duns = the schoolman Duns Scotus, whose name became synonymous with the most minute and pedantic textual study.
67 *trick . . . cards*: in the game of primero.

YOUNGEST SON. Stay, good authority's bastards; since I must
Through brothers' perjury die, O let me venom
Their souls with curses.
FIRST OFFICER. Come, 'tis no time to curse.
YOUNGEST SON. Must I bleed then without respect of sign? Well,
My fault was sweet sport, which the world approves:
I die for that which every woman loves.
Exeunt YOUNGEST SON *and officers.*

SCENE V

Enter VINDICE, *disguised, with* HIPPOLITO.

VINDICE. O sweet, delectable, rare, happy ravishing!
HIPPOLITO. Why, what's the matter, brother?
VINDICE. O, 'tis able
To make a man spring up and knock his forehead
Against yon silver ceiling.
HIPPOLITO. Prithee, tell me;
Why may not I partake with you? You vowed once
To give me share to every tragic thought.
VINDICE. By the mass, I think I did too:
Then I'll divide it to thee. The old duke,
Thinking my outward shape and inward heart
Are cut out of one piece (for he that prates his secrets,
His heart stands o'th'outside) hires me by price
To greet him with a lady
In some fit place veiled from the eyes o'th'court,
Some darkened, blushless angle that is guilty
Of his forefathers' lusts and great folks' riots;
To which I easily (to maintain my shape)
Consented, and did wish his impudent grace

---

78 'Must I have my blood drawn without consideration of whether the stars are auspicious for such an event?' This gloss seems more in keeping with the Youngest Son's mordant manner than Foakes's idea that 'respect of sign' = 'honour of some sign to mark the occasion'.

4 *silver ceiling*: (a) the sky, (b) the 'heavens' or canopy over the stage.

10 *prates*: blabs, displays.

14 *angle*: corner.

16 *shape*: disguise.

To meet her here in this unsunnèd lodge
Wherein 'tis night at noon; and here the rather
Because unto the torturing of his soul
The bastard and the duchess have appointed
Their meeting too in this luxurious circle;
Which most afflicting sight will kill his eyes
Before we kill the rest of him.

HIPPOLITO. 'Twill, i'faith! Most dreadfully digested!
I see not how you could have missed me, brother.

VINDICE. True, but the violence of my joy forgot it.

HIPPOLITO. Ay, but where's that lady now?

VINDICE. O, at that word
I'm lost again; you cannot find me yet;
I'm in a throng of happy apprehensions.
He's suited for a lady; I have took care
For a delicious lip, a sparkling eye:
You shall be witness brother.
Be ready; stand with your hat off. *Exit* VINDICE.

HIPPOLITO. Troth, I wonder what lady it should be?
Yet 'tis no wonder, now I think again,
To have a lady stoop to a duke, that stoops unto his men.
'Tis common to be common through the world,
And there's more private common shadowing vices
Than those who are known both by their names and prices.
'Tis part of my allegiance to stand bare
To the duke's concubine; and here she comes.

Enter VINDICE *with the masked skull of his love, dressed up in tires.*

VINDICE. (*to the skull*) Madam, his grace will not be absent long.
Secret? Ne'er doubt us, madam. 'Twill be worth
Three velvet gowns to your ladyship. Known?
Few ladies respect that disgrace: a poor thin shell!

---

25 *digested*: assimilated and worked out.
26 *missed me*: failed to think of me in connection with your plans.
29 *find me*: keep up with my witty plans.
30 *apprehensions*: witty ideas.
31 *suited for*: provided with.
42 s.d. *tires*: headdresses.

'Tis the best grace you have to do it well.
I'll save your hand that labour; I'll unmask you.
Reveals the skull.

HIPPOLITO. Why brother, brother!

VINDICE. Art thou beguiled now? Tut, a lady can
At such all hid beguile a wiser man.
Have I not fitted the old surfeiter
With a quaint piece of beauty? Age and bare bone
Are e'er allied in action. Here's an eye
Able to tempt a great man – to serve God;
A pretty hanging lip, that has forgot now to dissemble.
Methinks this mouth should make a swearer tremble,
A drunkard clasp his teeth and not undo 'em
To suffer wet damnation to run through 'em.
Here's a cheek keeps her colour, let the wind go
whistle;
Spout rain, we fear thee not; be hot or cold,
All's one with us. And is not he absurd
Whose fortunes are upon their faces set,
That fear no other god but wind and wet?

HIPPOLITO. Brother, y'ave spoke that right.
Is this the form that, living, shone so bright?

VINDICE. The very same.
And now methinks I could e'en chide myself
For doting on her beauty, though her death
Shall be revenged after no common action.
Does the silkworm expend her yellow labours
For thee? For thee does she undo herself?
Are lordships sold to maintain ladyships
For the poor benefit of a bewitching minute?
Why does yon fellow falsify highways,
And put his life between the judge's lips
To refine such a thing, keeps horse and men
To beat their valours for her?
Surely we're all mad people, and they

---

51 *all hid*: i.e. hide and seek.
53 *quaint piece*: fitting, suitable lady.
63 *set*: staked.
70 *after . . . action*: in no ordinary way.
75 A difficult line – I follow Gibbons in taking 'fellow' = 'highwayman' and 'falsify' = 'make unsafe'.
78 *beat their valours*: 'wear out their strengths' (Foakes).

Whom we think are, are not: we mistake those;
'Tis we are mad in sense, they but in clothes.
HIPPOLITO. Faith, and in clothes too we, give us our due.
VINDICE. Does every proud and self-affecting dame
Camphire her face for this? And grieve her Maker
In sinful baths of milk, when many an infant starves
For her superfluous outside: all for this?
Who now bids twenty pounds a night, prepares
Music, perfumes and sweetmeats? All are hushed;
Thou mayst lie chaste now! It were fine, methinks,
To have thee seen at revels, forgetful feasts
And unclean brothels; sure 'twould fright the sinner
And make him a good coward, put a reveller
Out of his antic amble
And cloy an epicure with empty dishes.
Here might a scornful and ambitious woman
Look through and through herself. See, ladies, with
false forms
You deceive men but cannot deceive worms. –
Now to my tragic business. Look you, brother,
I have not fashioned this only for show
And useless property; no, it shall bear a part
E'en in its own revenge. This very skull,
Whose mistress the duke poisoned, with this drug,
The mortal curse of the earth, shall be revenged
In the like strain and kiss his lips to death.
As much as the dumb thing can, he shall feel;
What fails in poison we'll supply in steel.
HIPPOLITO. Brother, I do applaud thy constant vengeance,
The quaintness of thy malice, above thought.
VINDICE *puts poison on the skull's mouth.*
VINDICE. So, 'tis laid on: now come and welcome, duke,
I have her for thee. I protest it, brother,
Methinks she makes almost as fair a fine

---

84 *Camphire*: wash her face with camphor (as a cosmetic).
86 *superfluous outside*: the idea is, I think, that many infants starve because the lady uses milk for washing flesh, which is 'superfluous' in the sense of transient and therefore not of primary importance.
93 *antic*: crazy, foolish.
100 *property*: as a stage-property.
108 *quaintness*: subtlety, wit.
111 *fine*: see Textual note, p. 195.

As some old gentlewoman in a periwig.
(*To the skull*) Hide thy face now for shame; thou hast need have a mask now.
'Tis vain when beauty flows, but when it fleets
This would become graves better than the streets.

HIPPOLITO. You have my voice in that.

Voices within.

Hark, the duke's come.

VINDICE. Peace, let's observe what company he brings,
And how he does absent 'em, for you know
He'll wish all private. Brother, fall you back a little
With the bony lady.

HIPPOLITO. That I will.

Withdraws.

VINDICE. So, so:
Now nine years' vengeance crowd into a minute!

Enter the DUKE *and gentlemen.*

DUKE. You shall have leave to leave us, with this charge,
Upon your lives, if we be missed by th'duchess
Or any of the nobles, to give out
We're privately rid forth.

VINDICE. (*aside*) O, happiness!

DUKE. With some few honourable gentlemen, you may say;
You may name those that are away from court.

FIRST GENTLEMAN. Your will and pleasure shall be done, my lord.

Exeunt gentlemen.

VINDICE. (*aside*) 'Privately rid forth'!
He strives to make sure work on't.

Advances.

Your good grace!

DUKE. Piato, well done, hast brought her? What lady is't?

VINDICE. Faith, my lord, a country lady, a little bashful at first, as most of them are, but after the first kiss, my lord, the worst is past with them. Your grace knows now what you have to do. Sh'as somewhat a grave look with her, but . . .

---

115 *fleets*: passes away.
119 *absent*: dismiss.
137 *grave*: (a) solemn, (b) pertaining to the grave.

DUKE. I love that best. Conduct her.
VINDICE. (*aside*) Have at all!
DUKE. In gravest looks the greatest faults seem less;
Give me that sin that's robed in holiness.
VINDICE. (*to Hippolito*) Back with the torch, brother; raise the perfumes.
DUKE. How sweet can a duke breathe! Age has no fault;
Pleasure should meet in a perfumèd mist. –
Lady, sweetly encountered. I came from court,
I must be bold with you.

Kisses the skull.

O, what's this? O!
VINDICE. Royal villain! White devil!
DUKE. O!
VINDICE. Brother,
Place the torch here, that his affrighted eyeballs
May start into those hollows. Duke, dost know
Yon dreadful vizard? View it well; 'tis the skull
Of Gloriana, whom thou poisoned'st last.
DUKE. O, 'tas poisoned me.
VINDICE. Didst not know that till now?
DUKE. What are you two?
VINDICE. Villains all three! The very raggèd bone
Has been sufficiently revenged.
DUKE. O, Hippolito, call treason.
HIPPOLITO. Yes, my good lord. Treason, treason, treason!

Stamping on him.

DUKE. Then I'm betrayed.
VINDICE. Alas, poor lecher, in the hands of knaves
A slavish duke is baser than his slaves.
DUKE. My teeth are eaten out.
VINDICE. Hadst any left?
HIPPOLITO. I think but few.
VINDICE. Then those that did eat are eaten.
DUKE. O, my tongue!
VINDICE. Your tongue? 'Twill teach you to kiss closer,
Not like a slobbering Dutchman. You have eyes still:

---

138 *Conduct*: summon.
142 *Age . . . fault*: There is no physical inadequacy with my old age.
144–5 See Textual note, p. 195.
150 *last*: some time ago.
164 *slobbering*: see Textual note, p. 195.

Look, monster, what a lady hast thou made me
My once-betrothed wife.

DUKE. Is it thou, villain?
Nay, then . . .

VINDICE. 'Tis I, 'tis Vindice, 'tis I!

HIPPOLITO. And let this comfort thee: our lord and father
Fell sick upon the infection of thy frowns
And died in sadness: be that thy hope of life.

DUKE. O!

VINDICE. He had his tongue, yet grief made him die speechless.
Pooh! 'Tis but early yet; now I'll begin
To stick thy soul with ulcers. I will make
Thy spirit grievous sore: it shall not rest
But like some pestilent man toss in thy breast.
Mark me, duke:
Thou'rt a renowned, high and mighty cuckold.

DUKE. O!

VINDICE. Thy bastard, thy bastard rides a-hunting in thy brow.

DUKE. Millions of deaths!

VINDICE. Nay, to afflict thee more,
Here in this lodge they meet for damnèd clips:
Those eyes shall see the incest of their lips.

DUKE. Is there a hell besides this, villains?

VINDICE. Villain?
Nay, heaven is just, scorns are the hires of scorns;
I ne'er knew yet adulterer without horns.

HIPPOLITO. Once ere they die 'tis quitted.

Music.

VINDICE. Hark, the music!
Their banquet is prepared, they're coming.

DUKE. O
Kill me not with that sight.

VINDICE. Thou shalt not lose
That sight for all thy dukedom.

DUKE. Traitors, murderers!

165–6 *what . . . wife*: what a lady you have made for me from the person I was once betrothed to.
172 This line refers to Vindice's father.
185 *hires*: recompenses.
187 *quitted*: requited.

VINDICE. What, is not thy tongue eaten out yet?
Then we'll invent a silence.
Brother, stifle the torch.
DUKE. Treason! Murder!
VINDICE. Nay, faith, we'll have you hushed. Now with thy dagger
Nail down his tongue, and mine shall keep possession
About his heart: if he but gasp he dies.
We dread not death to quittance injuries.
Brother, if he but wink, not brooking the foul object,
Let our two other hands tear up his lids
And make his eyes like comets shine through blood:
When the bad bleeds, then is the tragedy good.
HIPPOLITO. Whist, brother! Music's at our ear; they come.

Enter SPURIO *meeting the* DUCHESS.

SPURIO. Had not that kiss a taste of sin 'twere sweet.
DUCHESS. Why, there's no pleasure sweet but it is sinful.
SPURIO. True; such a bitter sweetness fate hath given,
Best side to us is the worst side to heaven.
DUCHESS. Push, come: 'tis the old duke, thy doubtful father,
The thought of him rubs heaven in thy way.
But I protest, by yonder waxen fire,
Forget him, or I'll poison him.
SPURIO. Madam, you urge a thought which ne'er had life;
So deadly do I loathe him for my birth
That if he took me hasped within his bed
I would add murder to adultery
And with my sword give up his years to death.
DUCHESS. Why, now thou'rt sociable; let's in and feast:
Loud'st music sound! Pleasure is banquet's guest.
Exeunt SPURIO *and the* DUCHESS.
DUKE. I cannot brook . . .
VINDICE *kills him.*

---

192 *invent*: create.
197 *quittance*: requite.
198 *brooking*: tolerating.
204 cp. Lussurioso, I.iii.105–6.
208 *rubs*: revives in your mind.
209 *waxen fire*: candle.
213 *hasped*: in coition.

VINDICE. The brook is turned to blood.
HIPPOLITO. Thanks to loud music.
VINDICE. 'Twas our friend indeed.
'Tis state in music for a duke to bleed.
The dukedom wants a head, though yet unknown:
As fast as they peep up, let's cut 'em down.
Exeunt VINDICE *and* HIPPOLITO.

SCENE VI

Enter the duchess's two sons, AMBITIOSO *and* SUPERVACUO.

AMBITIOSO. Was not his execution rarely plotted?
We are the duke's sons now.
SUPERVACUO. Ay, you may thank my policy for that.
AMBITIOSO. Your policy for what?
SUPERVACUO. Why, was't not my invention, brother,
To slip the judges? And in lesser compass
Did I not draw the model of his death,
Advising you to sudden officers
And e'en extemporal execution?
AMBITIOSO. Heart, 'twas a thing I thought on too.
SUPERVACUO. Thou thought on't too? 'Sfoot, slander not your thoughts
With glorious untruth; I know 'twas from you.
AMBITIOSO. Sir, I say 'twas in my head.
SUPERVACUO. Ay, like your brains then,
Ne'er to come out as long as you lived.
AMBITIOSO. You'd have the honour on't, forsooth, that your wit
Led him to the scaffold.
SUPERVACUO. Since it is my due
I'll publish it, but I'll ha't in spite of you.
AMBITIOSO. Methinks y'are much too bold; you should a little
Remember us, brother, next to be honest duke.

---

3 *policy*: clever plotting.
6 *slip*: bypass.
8 *sudden*: swift in action.
9 *extemporal*: immediate.
12 *from you*: not in your mind.
19 *honest*: regarded with honour; perhaps also in the normal sense, but ironically.

SUPERVACUO. (*aside*) Ay, it shall be as easy for you to be duke
As to be honest, and that's never, i'faith.
AMBITIOSO. Well, cold he is by this time, and because
We're both ambitious, be it our amity,
And let the glory be shared equally.
SUPERVACUO. I am content to that.
AMBITIOSO. This night our younger brother shall out of prison.
I have a trick.
SUPERVACUO. A trick? Prithee, what is't?
AMBITIOSO. We'll get him out by a wile.
SUPERVACUO. Prithee, what wile?
AMBITIOSO. No, sir, you shall not know it 'til't be done;
For then you'd swear 'twere yours.

Enter an officer, with a head.

SUPERVACUO. How now, what's he?
AMBITIOSO. One of the officers.
SUPERVACUO. Desired news.
AMBITIOSO. How now, my friend?
OFFICER. My lords, under your pardon, I am allotted
To that desertless office to present you
With the yet bleeding head.
SUPERVACUO. (*aside*) Ha, ha, excellent.
AMBITIOSO. (*to Supervacuo*) All's sure our own. Brother, canst weep, think'st thou?
'Twould grace our flattery much. Think of some dame:
'Twill teach thee to dissemble.
SUPERVACUO. (*to Ambitioso*) I have thought;
Now for yourself.
AMBITIOSO. Our sorrows are so fluent,
Our eyes o'erflow our tongues; words spoke in tears
Are like the murmurs of the waters: the sound
Is loudly heard but cannot be distinguished.
SUPERVACUO. How died he, pray?
OFFICER. O, full of rage and spleen.
SUPERVACUO. He died most valiantly, then; we're glad
To hear it.
OFFICER. We could not woo him once to pray.

---

34 *desertless*: thankless, unrewarding.

AMBITIOSO. He showed himself a gentleman in that,
Give him his due.
OFFICER. But in the stead of prayer
He drew forth oaths.
SUPERVACUO. Then he did pray, dear heart,
Although you understood him not.
OFFICER. My lords,
E'en at his last, with pardon be it spoke,
He cursed you both.
SUPERVACUO. He cursed us? 'Las, good soul.
AMBITIOSO. It was not in our powers, but the duke's
pleasure.
(*Aside*) Finely dissembled o'both sides, sweet fate,
O happy opportunity!

Enter LUSSURIOSO.

LUSSURIOSO. Now, my lords . . .
BOTH. O!
LUSSURIOSO. Why do you shun me, brothers?
You may come nearer now:
The savour of the prison has forsook me.
I thank such kind lords as yourselves, I'm free.
AMBITIOSO. Alive!
SUPERVACUO. In health!
AMBITIOSO. Released!
We were both e'en amazed with joy to see it.
LUSSURIOSO. I am much to thank you.
SUPERVACUO. Faith, we spared no tongue unto my lord
the duke.
AMBITIOSO. I know your delivery, brother,
Had not been half so sudden but for us.
SUPERVACUO. O how we pleaded!
LUSSURIOSO. Most deserving brothers,
In my best studies I will think of it.
Exit LUSSURIOSO.
AMBITIOSO. O death and vengeance!
SUPERVACUO. Hell and torments!
AMBITIOSO. Slave, cam'st thou to delude us?
OFFICER. Delude you, my lords?
SUPERVACUO. Ay, villain; where's this head now?

---

47 *stead*: place.
57 *savour*: smell.

OFFICER. Why, here, my lord.
Just after his delivery, you came
With warrant from the duke to behead your brother.
AMBITIOSO. Ay, our brother, the duke's son.
OFFICER. The duke's son,
My lord, had his release before you came.
AMBITIOSO. Whose head's that then?
OFFICER. His whom you left command for,
Your own brother's.
AMBITIOSO. Our brother's? O furies!
SUPERVACUO. Plagues!
AMBITIOSO. Confusions!
SUPERVACUO. Darkness!
AMBITIOSO. Devils!
SUPERVACUO. Fell it out so accursedly?
AMBITIOSO. So damnedly?
SUPERVACUO. Villain, I'll brain thee with it!
OFFICER. O my good lord!
SUPERVACUO. The devil overtake thee!

Exit officer.

AMBITIOSO. O fatal!
SUPERVACUO. O prodigious to our bloods!
AMBITIOSO. Did we dissemble?
SUPERVACUO. Did we make our tears women for thee?
AMBITIOSO. Laugh and rejoice for thee?
SUPERVACUO. Bring warrant for thy death?
AMBITIOSO. Mock off thy head?
SUPERVACUO. You had a trick, you had a wile, forsooth.
AMBITIOSO. A murrain meet 'em! There's none of these wiles that ever came to good. I see now there is nothing sure in mortality but mortality.
Well, no more words; shalt be revenged, i'faith.
Come, throw off clouds now, brother; think of vengeance
And deeper-settled hate. Sirrah, sit fast,
We'll pull down all, but thou shalt down at last.

Exeunt AMBITIOSO *and* SUPERVACUO.

---

80 *prodigious*: ominous.
85 *murrain*: plague (strictly, a cattle disease).
90 *Sirrah*: aimed at Lussurioso.

ACT IV

SCENE I

Enter LUSSURIOSO *with* HIPPOLITO.

LUSSURIOSO. Hippolito.
HIPPOLITO. My lord, has your good lordship
Aught to command me in?
LUSSURIOSO. I prithee leave us.
HIPPOLITO. (*aside*) How's this? Come and leave us?
LUSSURIOSO. Hippolito.
HIPPOLITO. Your honour,
I stand ready for any duteous employment.
LUSSURIOSO. Heart, what mak'st thou here?
HIPPOLITO. (*aside*) A pretty lordly humour;
He bids me to be present to depart; something
Has stung his honour.
LUSSURIOSO. Be nearer, draw nearer.
Ye are not so good, methinks. I'm angry with you.
HIPPOLITO. With me, my lord? I'm angry with myself for't.
LUSSURIOSO. You did prefer a goodly fellow to me:
'Twas wittily elected, 'twas. I thought
H'ad been a villain and he proves a knave,
To me a knave!
HIPPOLITO. I chose him for the best, my lord.
'Tis much my sorrow if neglect in him
Breed discontent in you.
LUSSURIOSO. Neglect? 'Twas will!
Judge of it:
Firmly to tell of an incredible act –
Not to be thought, less to be spoken of –
'Twixt my stepmother and the bastard: O,
Incestuous sweets between 'em.
HIPPOLITO. Fie, my lord!
LUSSURIOSO. I, in kind loyalty to my father's forehead,
Made this a desperate arm, and in that fury
Committed treason on the lawful bed

---

2 See Textual note, p. 195.
12 *elected*: chosen.
16 *will*: deliberate intention.

And with my sword e'en raced my father's bosom,
For which I was within a stroke of death.
HIPPOLITO. Alack, I'm sorry.

Enter VINDICE, *disguised.*

(*Aside*) 'Sfoot, just upon the stroke
Jars in my brother; 'twill be villainous music.
VINDICE. My honoured lord.
LUSSURIOSO. Away!
Prithee forsake us – hereafter we'll not know thee.
VINDICE. Not know me, my lord? Your lordship cannot choose.
LUSSURIOSO. Begone, I say; thou art a false knave.
VINDICE. Why, the easier to be known, my lord.
LUSSURIOSO. Push, I shall prove too bitter with a word,
Make thee a perpetual prisoner
And lay this ironage upon thee.
VINDICE. (*aside*) Mum,
For there's a doom would make a woman dumb.
Missing the bastard, next him: the wind's come about –
Now 'tis my brother's turn to stay, mine to go out.
Exit VINDICE.
LUSSURIOSO. H'as greatly moved me.
HIPPOLITO. Much to blame, i'faith.
LUSSURIOSO. But I'll recover, to his ruin. 'Twas told me lately, I know not whether falsely, that you'd a brother.
HIPPOLITO. Who, I? Yes, my good lord, I have a brother.
LUSSURIOSO. How chance the court ne'er saw him? Of what nature?
How does he apply his hours?
HIPPOLITO. Faith, to curse fates
Who, as he thinks, ordained him to be poor:

---

25 *raced*: grazed.
28 *Jars in*: the verb has the sense of 'comes in like discordant music': Vindice's entry is at just the wrong stroke of time and the result will be 'villainous music'.
30 *forsake*: leave.
36 *ironage*: (a) collection of iron fetters: (b) the iron age, fourth, last and worst of the ages of classical mythology; a period marked by vice and brutality.
Mum: silence.
47 *ordained*: predetermined.

Keeps at home, full of want and discontent.
LUSSURIOSO. (*aside*) There's hope in him, for discontent and want
Is the best clay to mould a villain of. –
Hippolito, wish him to repair to us:
If there be aught in him to please our blood
For thy sake we'll advance him, and build fair
His meanest fortunes; for it is in us
To rear up towers from cottages.
HIPPOLITO. It is so, my lord. He will attend your honour,
But he's a man in whom much melancholy dwells.
LUSSURIOSO. Why, the better; bring him to court.
HIPPOLITO. With willingness and speed.
(*Aside*) Whom he cast off e'en now, must now succeed.
Brother, disguise must off;
In thine own shape now I'll prefer thee to him:
How strangely does himself work to undo him.
Exit HIPPOLITO.
LUSSURIOSO. This fellow will come fitly: he shall kill
That other slave that did abuse my spleen
And made it swell to treason. I have put
Much of my heart into him – he must die.
He that knows great men's secrets and proves slight,
That man ne'er lives to see his beard turn white.
Ay, he shall speed him: I'll employ thee, brother;
Slaves are but nails to drive out one another.
He being of black condition, suitable
To want and ill content, hope of preferment
Will grind him to an edge.

The nobles enter.

FIRST NOBLE. Good days unto your honour.
LUSSURIOSO. My kind lords, I do return the like.
SECOND NOBLE. Saw you my lord the duke?
LUSSURIOSO. My lord and father?

---

51 *repair*: report, come to see.
64 *fitly*: at the right time.
65 *spleen*: anger.
66–7 *I . . . into*: I have confided a great deal to him.
68 *slight*: unreliable.
70 *speed*: kill.
72 *black condition*: melancholic.
74 s.d. See Textual note, p. 195.

Is he from court?
FIRST NOBLE. He's sure from court.
But where, which way his pleasure took we know not,
Nor can we hear on't.
LUSSURIOSO. Here comes those should tell.

Enter the duke's gentlemen.

Saw you my lord and father?
FIRST GENTLEMAN. Not since two hours before noon, my lord,
And then he privately rid forth.
LUSSURIOSO. O, he's rode forth?
FIRST NOBLEMAN. 'Twas wondrous privately.
SECOND NOBLEMAN. There's none i'th'court had any knowledge on't.
LUSSURIOSO. His grace is old and sudden; 'tis no treason
To say the duke my father has a humour,
Or such a toy about him – what in us
Would appear light, in him seems virtuous.
FIRST GENTLEMAN. 'Tis oracle, my lord.

Exeunt all.

SCENE II

Enter VINDICE *and* HIPPOLITO*;* VINDICE *out of his disguise.*

HIPPOLITO. So, so, all's as it should be – y'are yourself.
VINDICE. How that great villain puts me to my shifts.
HIPPOLITO. He that did lately in disguise reject thee
Shall, now thou art thyself, as much respect thee.
VINDICE. 'Twill be the quainter fallacy. But, brother,
'Sfoot, what use will he put me to now, think'st thou?
HIPPOLITO. Nay, you must pardon me in that – I know not.
H'as some employment for you, but what 'tis

---

86 *sudden*: impetuous.
87 *humour*: whim.
88 *toy*: idle fancy.
89 *light*: frivolous.
90 *oracle*: absolute truth.
2 *shifts*: changes of disguises or roles.
5 *quainter*: wittier.
fallacy: deception.

He and his secretary the devil knows best.
VINDICE. Well, I must suit my tongue to his desires,
What colour soe'er they be, hoping at last
To pile up all my wishes on his breast.
HIPPOLITO. Faith, brother, he himself shows the way.
VINDICE. Now the duke is dead the realm is clad in clay.
His death being yet unknown, under his name
The people still are governed. Well, thou his son
Art not long-lived: thou shalt not joy his death.
To kill thee, then, I should most honour thee,
For 'twould stand firm in every man's belief,
Thou'st a kind child and only died'st with grief.
HIPPOLITO. You fetch about well, but let's talk in present.
How will you appear in fashion different,
As well as in apparel, to make all things possible?
If you be but once tripped, we fall forever.
It is not the least policy to be doubtful:
You must change tongue: familiar was your first.
VINDICE. Why, I'll bear me in some strain of melancholy
And string myself with heavy-sounding wire,
Like such an instrument
That speaks merry things sadly.
HIPPOLITO. Then 'tis as I meant:
I gave you out at first in discontent.
VINDICE. I'll turn myself and then . . .

Enter LUSSURIOSO.

HIPPOLITO. 'Sfoot, here he comes;
Hast thought upon't?
VINDICE. Salute him, fear not me.
LUSSURIOSO. Hippolito.
HIPPOLITO. Your lordship?
LUSSURIOSO. What's he yonder?
HIPPOLITO. 'Tis Vindice, my discontented brother,
Whom, 'cording to your will, I've brought to court.

---

9 *secretary*: confidant.
14 *clad in clay*: buried (Vindice is saying that the old régime has died with the old duke).
20 *kind*: natural.
21 *fetch about*: wander around the main point.
24 *tripped*: caught out.
25 *doubtful*: careful.
32 *turn*: transform.

LUSSURIOSO. Is that thy brother? Beshrew me, a good presence.
I wonder h'as been from the court so long. –
Come nearer.
HIPPOLITO. Brother, lord Lussurioso, the duke's son.
LUSSURIOSO. Be more near us; welcome; nearer yet.

VINDICE *snatches off his hat and makes legs to him.*

VINDICE. How don you? God you good den.
LUSSURIOSO. We thank thee.
How strangely such a coarse, homely salute
Shows in the palace, where we greet in fire,
Nimble and desperate tongues. Should we name
God in a salutation 'twould ne'er be stood on – heaven!
Tell me what has made thee so melancholy?
VINDICE. Why, going to law.
LUSSURIOSO. Why, will that make a man melancholy?
VINDICE. Yes, to look upon ink and black buckram. I went me to law in 'Anno quadragesimo secundo', and I waded out of it in 'Anno sextagesimo tertio'.
LUSSURIOSO. What, three and twenty years in law?
VINDICE. I have known those that have been five and fifty, and all about pullen and pigs.
LUSSURIOSO. May it be possible such men should breathe
To vex the terms so much?
VINDICE. 'Tis food to some, my lord.
There are old men at the present that are so poisoned with the affectation of law-words (having had many suits canvassed) that their common talk is nothing but Barbary Latin. They cannot so much as pray but in

---

41 s.d. *makes legs*: bows.
42 *don*: do (= are).
den: evening. Vindice is using deliberately archaic–rustic word-forms.
46 *'twould . . . on*: no one would worry about the propriety.
50 *black buckram*: an attorney's bag.
51 *'Anno . . . secundo'*: 42nd year (of an imagined reign).
52 *'Anno . . . tertio'*: 63rd year.
53 Lussurioso's arithmetic is faulty.
55 *pullen*: poultry (again rustic).
57 *terms*: the periods when the law-courts are in session.
61 *Barbary Latin*: bad (barbarous) Latin.

law, that their sins may be removed with a writ of error, and their souls fetched up to heaven with a sasarara.

LUSSURIOSO. It seems most strange to me;
Yet all the world meets round in the same bent;
Where the heart's set, there goes the tongue's consent.
How dost apply thy studies, fellow?

VINDICE. Study?
Why, to think how a great man lies a-dying and a poor cobbler tolls the bell for him. How he cannot depart the world and see the great chest stand before him; when he lies speechless, how he will point you readily to all the boxes; and when he is past all memory, as the gossips guess, then thinks he of forfeitures and obligations; nay, when to all men's hearings he whurls and rattles in the throat, he's busy threat'ning his poor tenants. And this would last me now some seven years' thinking or thereabouts. But I have a conceit a-coming in picture upon this. I draw it myself, which i'faith, la, I'll present to your honour; you shall not choose but like it, for your lordship shall give me nothing for it.

LUSSURIOSO. Nay, you mistake me then,
For I am published bountiful enough.
Let's taste of your conceit.

VINDICE. In picture, my lord?

LUSSURIOSO. Ay, in picture.

VINDICE. Marry, this is it:
'A usuring father, to be boiling in hell, and his son and heir with a whore dancing over him.'

HIPPOLITO. (*aside*) H'as pared him to the quick.

62–3 *writ of error*: a writ brought to secure a reversal of judgement on the grounds of error in the original judgement.

64 *sasarara*: = 'certiorari': a writ from an upper court arising from a complaint that the person concerned failed to find justice in a lower court.

65 See Textual note, p. 195.

66 *bent*: curves.

74 *forfeitures*: deprivations of life, estates etc. as result of a crime.

75 *obligations*: enforceable agreements binding a person to pay a sum of money or fulfil a specified task.

85 *in picture*: as a pictorial emblem.

90 *pared . . . quick*: the conceit reflects Lussurioso's position exactly.

LUSSURIOSO. The conceit's pretty, i'faith,
But take't upon my life 'twill ne'er be liked.

VINDICE. No? Why, I'm sure the whore will be liked well enough.

HIPPOLITO. (*aside*) Ay, if she were out o'th'picture, he'd like her then himself.

VINDICE. And as for the son and heir he shall be an eye-sore to no young revellers, for he shall be drawn in cloth of gold breeches.

LUSSURIOSO. And thou hast put my meaning in the pockets
And canst not draw that out! My thought was this:
To see the picture of a usuring father
Boiling in hell, our rich men would ne'er like it.

VINDICE. O true, I cry you heartily mercy. I know the reason, for some of 'em had rather be damned indeed than damned in colours.

LUSSURIOSO. (*aside*) A parlous melancholy! H'as wit enough
To murder any man, and I'll give him means. –
I think thou art ill-monied?

VINDICE. Money? Ho, ho!
'T'as been my want so long 'tis now my scoff;
I've e'en forgot what colour silver's of.

LUSSURIOSO. (*aside*) It hits as I could wish.

VINDICE. I get good clothes
Of those that dread my humour, and for table-room
I feed on those that cannot be rid of me.

LUSSURIOSO. Somewhat to set thee up withal.

Gives him gold.

VINDICE. O, mine eyes!

LUSSURIOSO. How now, man?

VINDICE. Almost struck blind.
This bright unusual shine to me seems proud;
I dare not look till the sun be in a cloud.

LUSSURIOSO. (*aside*) I think I shall affect his melancholy. –
How are they now?

---

100 *pockets*: see Textual note, p. 196.
106 *damned in colours*: have their vices presented in a picture.
107 *parlous*: keen, dangerous.
117 *proud*: magnificent.

VINDICE. The better for your asking.
LUSSURIOSO. You shall be better yet if you but fasten
Truly on my intent. Now y'are both present
I will unbrace such a close private villain
Unto your vengeful swords, the like ne'er heard of,
Who hath disgraced you much and injured us.
HIPPOLITO. Disgraced us, my lord?
LUSSURIOSO. Ay, Hippolito.
I kept it here till now that both your angers
Might meet him at once.
VINDICE. I'm covetous.
To know the villain.
LUSSURIOSO. (*to Hippolito*) You know him – that slave pander
Piato, whom we threatened last
With irons in perpetual 'prisonment.
VINDICE. (*aside*) All this is I.
HIPPOLITO. Is't he, my lord?
LUSSURIOSO. I'll tell you:
You first preferred him to me.
VINDICE. Did you, brother?
HIPPOLITO. I did indeed.
LUSSURIOSO. And the ingrateful villain,
To quit that kindness, strongly wrought with me –
Being, as you see, a likely man for pleasure –
With jewels to corrupt your virgin sister.
HIPPOLITO. O villain!
VINDICE. He shall surely die that did it.
LUSSURIOSO. I, far from thinking any virgin harm,
Especially knowing her to be as chaste
As that part which scarce suffers to be touched,
Th'eye, would not endure him.
VINDICE. Would you not, my lord?
'Twas wondrous honourably done.
LUSSURIOSO. But with some fine frowns kept him out.
VINDICE. Out, slave!
LUSSURIOSO. What did he me but in revenge of that
Went of his own free will to make infirm
Your sister's honour, whom I honour with my soul

123 *unbrace*: reveal.
135 *quit*: repay.
138 *He . . . it*: Vindice's remark is neatly ironical – the doer is, of course, Lussurioso, who is to die for his vice.

For chaste respect; and not prevailing there
(As 'twas but desperate folly to attempt it)
In mere spleen, by the way, waylays your mother,
Whose honour being a coward, as it seems,
Yielded by little force.

VINDICE. Coward indeed.

LUSSURIOSO. He, proud of their advantage, as he thought,
Brought me these news for happy, but I – heaven
Forgive me for't –

VINDICE. What did your honour?

LUSSURIOSO. In rage pushed him from me,
Trampled beneath his throat, spurned him and bruised:
Indeed I was too cruel, to say troth.

HIPPOLITO. Most nobly managed!

VINDICE. (*aside*) Has not heaven an ear? Is all the lightning wasted?

LUSSURIOSO. If I now were so impatient in a modest cause,
What should you be?

VINDICE. Full mad: he shall not live
To see the moon change.

LUSSURIOSO. He's about the palace.
Hippolito, entice him this way that thy brother
May take full mark of him.

HIPPOLITO. Heart! That shall not need, my lord;
I can direct him so far.

LUSSURIOSO. Yet for my hate's sake,
Go, wind him this way: I'll see him bleed myself.

HIPPOLITO. (*to Vindice*) What now, brother?

VINDICE. Nay, e'en what you will: y'are put to it, brother!

HIPPOLITO. An impossible task, I'll swear.
To bring him hither that's already here.

Exit HIPPOLITO.

LUSSURIOSO. Thy name? I have forgot it.

VINDICE. Vindice, my lord.

---

149 *chaste respect*: respect for chastity.
151 *spleen*: caprice, or frustration.
154 *their*: I follow Ross in taking this to refer to 'these news' (l. 155).
162 *modest cause*: (a) a matter to do with sexual modesty; (b) one of little direct relevance to myself.
166 *full mark*: close look.
169 *wind*: draw, entice.

LUSSURIOSO. 'Tis a good name that.
VINDICE. Ay, a revenger.
LUSSURIOSO. It does betoken courage; thou shouldst be valiant
And kill thine enemies.
VINDICE. That's my hope, my lord.
LUSSURIOSO. This slave is one.
VINDICE. I'll doom him.
LUSSURIOSO. Then I'll praise thee!
Do thou observe me best, and I'll best raise thee.

Enter HIPPOLITO.

VINDICE. Indeed, I thank you.
LUSSURIOSO. Now, Hippolito, where's the slave pander?
HIPPOLITO. Your good lordship would have
A loathsome sight of him, much offensive.
He's not in case now to be seen, my lord:
The worst of all the deadly sins is in him,
That beggarly damnation, drunkenness.
LUSSURIOSO. Then he's a double slave.
VINDICE. (*to Hippolito*) 'Twas well conveyed;
Upon a sudden wit.
LUSSURIOSO. What, are you both
Firmly resolved? I'll see him dead myself.
VINDICE. Or else let us not live.
LUSSURIOSO. You may direct
Your brother to take note of him.
HIPPOLITO. I shall.
LUSSURIOSO. Rise but in this and you shall never fall.
VINDICE. Your honour's vassals.
LUSSURIOSO. (*aside*) This was wisely carried.
Deep policy in us makes fools of such:
Then must a slave die when he knows too much.

Exit LUSSURIOSO.

VINDICE. O, thou almighty patience! 'Tis my wonder
That such a fellow, impudent and wicked,
Should not be cloven as he stood,
Or with a secret wind burst open!
Is there no thunder left, or is't kept up

---

179 *observe*: attend me carefully.
184 *in case*: in a state.
187 *conveyed*: managed.

In stock for heavier vengeance? (*Thunder*) There it goes!
HIPPOLITO. Brother, we lose ourselves.
VINDICE. But I have found it.
'Twill hold, 'tis sure, thanks, thanks to any spirit
That mingled it 'mongst my inventions.
HIPPOLITO. What is't?
VINDICE. 'Tis sound and good; thou shalt partake it.
I'm hired to kill myself.
HIPPOLITO. True.
VINDICE. Prithee mark it;
And the old duke being dead but not conveyed;
For he's already missed too, and you know
Murder will peep out of the closest husk.
HIPPOLITO. Most true.
VINDICE. What say you then to this device?
If we dressed up the body of the duke . . .
HIPPOLITO. In that disguise of yours.
VINDICE. Y'are quick, y'ave reached it.
HIPPOLITO. I like it wondrously.
VINDICE. And being in drink, as you have published him,
To lean him on his elbow as if sleep had caught him,
Which claims most interest in such sluggy men.
HIPPOLITO. Good yet, but here's a doubt:
We, thought by th'duke's son to kill that pander,
Shall, when he is known, be thought to kill the duke.
VINDICE. Neither, O thanks, it is substantial:
For that disguise being on him which I wore it will be thought that I, which he calls the pander, did kill the duke and fled away in his apparel, leaving him so disguised to avoid swift pursuit.
HIPPOLITO. Firmer and firmer.
VINDICE. Nay, doubt not 'tis in grain;
I warrant it hold colour.

---

202 Hippolito is worried that the situation is getting beyond them; Vindice, however, has already thought out a stratagem.
207 *conveyed*: disposed of.
216 *sluggy*: sluggish.
218 *We*: see Textual note, p. 196.
220 *substantial*: firmly based (i.e. the whole plot is carefully thought out).
225 *in grain*: fast dyed (= substantial) so that the colour will not run (I.226).

HIPPOLITO. Let's about it.
VINDICE. But by the way too, now I think on't, brother,
Let's conjure that base devil out of our mother.
Exeunt VINDICE *and* HIPPOLITO.

SCENE III

Enter the DUCHESS *arm in arm with* SPURIO. *He seemeth lasciviously to her. After them enter* SUPERVACUO *running with a rapier; his brother* AMBITIOSO *stops him.*

SPURIO. Madam, unlock yourself; should it be seen,
Your arm would be suspected.
DUCHESS. Who is't that dares suspect or this or these?
May we not deal our favours where we please?
SPURIO. I'm confident you may.
Exeunt SPURIO *and the* DUCHESS.
AMBITIOSO. 'Sfoot, brother, hold.
SUPERVACUO. Would let the bastard shame us?
AMBITIOSO. Hold, hold, brother!
There's fitter time than now.
SUPERVACUO. Now, when I see it.
AMBITIOSO. 'Tis too much seen already.
SUPERVACUO. Seen and known.
The nobler she's the baser is she grown.
AMBITIOSO. If she were bent lasciviously, the fault
Of mighty women that sleep soft, O death,
Must she needs choose such an unequal sinner
To make all worse?
SUPERVACUO. A bastard, the duke's bastard!
Shame heaped on shame.
AMBITIOSO. O our disgrace!
Most women have small waist the world throughout,
But their desires are thousand miles about.
SUPERVACUO. Come, stay not here, let's after and prevent,
Or else they'll sin faster than we'll repent.
Exeunt AMBITIOSO *and* SUPERVACUO.

---

1 *unlock*: remove your arm from mine.
12 *unequal*: in status.

SCENE IV

Enter VINDICE *and* HIPPOLITO *bringing out their mother, one by one shoulder, and the other by the other, with daggers in their hands.*

VINDICE. O thou, for whom no name is bad enough!
GRATIANA. What means my sons? What, will you murder me?
VINDICE. Wicked, unnatural parent.
HIPPOLITO. Friend of women.
GRATIANA. O, are sons turned monsters? Help!
VINDICE. In vain.
GRATIANA. Are you so barbarous to set iron nipples
Upon the breast that gave you suck?
VINDICE. That breast
Is turned to quarled poison.
GRATIANA. Cut not your days for't: am not I your mother?
VINDICE. Thou dost usurp that title now by fraud,
For in that shell of mother breeds a bawd.
GRATIANA. A bawd? O name far loathsomer than hell.
HIPPOLITO. It should be so, knew'st thou thy office well.
GRATIANA. I hate it.
VINDICE. Ah, is't possible, you powers on high,
That women should dissemble when they die?
GRATIANA. Dissemble?
VINDICE. Did not the duke's son direct
A fellow of the world's condition hither
That did corrupt all that was good in thee?
Made thee uncivilly forget thyself
And work our sister to his lust?
GRATIANA. Who, I?
That had been monstrous! I defy that man
For any such intent. None lives so pure,
But shall be soiled with slander.
Good son, believe it not.

5–6 Gratiana refers, it seems, to the daggers having been pointed to her breast.
7 *quarled*: curdled.
8 See *Exodus* 20:12 for the biblical background to this remark.
12 *office*: duty, role.
14 *you powers*: see Textual note, p. 196.
20 *work*: manipulate, fashion.

VINDICE. O, I'm in doubt
Whether I'm myself or no! –
Stay, let me look again upon this face.
Who shall be saved when mothers have no grace?
HIPPOLITO. 'Twould make one half despair.
VINDICE. I was the man:
Defy me now! Let's see, do it modestly.
GRATIANA. O hell unto my soul.
VINDICE. In that disguise I, sent from the duke's son,
Tried you and found you base metal,
As any villain might have done.
GRATIANA. O no,
No tongue but yours could have bewitched me so.
VINDICE. O nimble in damnation, quick in tune:
There is no devil could strike fire so soon!
I am confuted in a word.
GRATIANA. O sons, forgive me! To myself I'll prove more true:
You that should honour me, I kneel to you.
Kneels and weeps.
VINDICE. A mother to give aim to her own daughter!
HIPPOLITO. True, brother; how far beyond nature 'tis,
Though many mothers do't.
VINDICE. Nay, and you draw tears once, go you to bed.
Wet will make iron blush and change to red:
Brother, it rains – 'twill spoil your dagger; house it.
HIPPOLITO. 'Tis done.
VINDICE. I'faith, 'tis a sweet shower, it does much good:
The fruitful grounds and meadows of her soul
Has been long dry. Pour down thou blessèd dew.
Rise mother; troth, this shower has made you higher.
GRATIANA. O you heavens!
Take this infectious spot out of my soul:
I'll rinse it in seven waters of mine eyes,
Make my tears salt enough to taste of grace:
To weep is to our sex naturally given,
But to weep truly, that's a gift from heaven.
VINDICE. Nay, I'll kiss you now. Kiss her, brother.

---

40 *give aim to*: a term from archery, here meaning 'direct someone to'.

51–6 Ross points out that this speech has the Protestant emphasis on 'the inseparability of "true" repentance from faith'.

Let's marry her to our souls, wherein's no lust,
And honourably love her.
HIPPOLITO. Let it be.
VINDICE. For honest women are so seld and rare
'Tis good to cherish those poor few that are.
O, you of easy wax, do but imagine,
Now the disease has left you, how leprously
That office would have clinged unto your forehead.
All mothers that had any graceful hue
Would have worn masks to hide their face at you.
It would have grown to this: at your foul name,
Green-coloured maids would have turned red with
shame.
HIPPOLITO. And then our sister, full of hire and baseness.
VINDICE. There had been boiling lead again:
The duke's son's great concubine!
A drab of state, a cloth o'silver slut,
To have her train borne up and her soul trail i'th'dirt:
Great . . .
HIPPOLITO. To be miserably great: rich to be
Eternally wretched.
VINDICE. O common madness.
Ask but the thriving'st harlot in cold blood,
She'd give the world to make her honour good.
Perhaps you'll say, but only to the duke's son,
In private. Why, she first begins with one
Who afterward to thousand proves a whore:
'Break ice in one place, it will crack in more.'
GRATIANA. Most certainly applied.
HIPPOLITO. O brother, you forget our business.
VINDICE. And well remembered. Joy's a subtle elf;
I think man's happiest when he forgets himself.
Farewell, once dried, now holy-watered mead;
Our hearts wear feathers that before wore lead.
GRATIANA. I'll give you this: that one I never knew
Plead better for and 'gainst the devil than you.
VINDICE. You make me proud on't.

---

60 *seld*: seldom found.
68 *Green-coloured*: immature, young.
69 *hire*: payment for (sexual) use.
82 'Most appropriate to this moment'.
86 *mead*: meadow.

HIPPOLITO. Commend us in all virtue to our sister.
VINDICE. Ay, for the love of heaven, to that true maid.
GRATIANA. With my best words.
VINDICE. Why, that was motherly said.
Exeunt VINDICE *and* HIPPOLITO.
GRATIANA. I wonder now what fury did transport me?
I feel good thoughts begin to settle in me.
O, with what forehead can I look on her
Whose honour I've so impiously beset?

Enter CASTIZA.

And here she comes.
CASTIZA. Now, mother, you have wrought with me so strongly
That what for my advancement, as to calm
The trouble of your tongue, I am content.
GRATIANA. Content to what?
CASTIZA. To do as you have wished me;
To prostitute my breast to the duke's son,
And put myself to common usury.
GRATIANA. I hope you will not so.
CASTIZA. Hope you I will not?
That's not the hope you look to be saved in.
GRATIANA. Truth, but it is.
CASTIZA. Do not deceive yourself:
I am, as you e'en, out of marble wrought.
What would you now? Are ye not pleased yet with me?
You shall not wish me to be more lascivious
Than I intend to be.
GRATIANA. Strike me not cold.
CASTIZA. How often have you charged me on your blessing
To be a cursèd woman? When you knew
Your blessing had no force to make me lewd
You laid your curse upon me: that did more.
The mother's curse is heavy: where that fights
Sons set in storm and daughters lose their lights.
GRATIANA. Good child, dear maid, if there be any spark
Of heavenly intellectual fire within thee,

---

96 *forehead*: countenance, expression.
104 *usury*: here, prostitution.
112 *charged*: ordered.
117 *Sons . . . storm*: punning on sons/suns.
119 *intellectual*: here, spiritual.

O let my breath revive it to a flame!
Put not all out with woman's wilful follies:
I am recovered of that foul disease
That haunts too many mothers; kind, forgive me,
Make me not sick in health. If then
My words prevailed when they were wickedness,
How much more now when they are just and good?

CASTIZA. I wonder what you mean? Are not you she
For whose infect persuasions I could scarce
Kneel out my prayers, and had much ado
In three hours' reading to untwist so much
Of the black serpent as you wound about me?

GRATIANA. 'Tis unfruitful, held tedious, to repeat what's past.
I'm now your present mother.

CASTIZA. Push, now 'tis too late.

GRATIANA. Bethink again, thou know'st not what thou say'st.

CASTIZA. No? 'Deny advancement, treasure, the duke's son!'

GRATIANA. O see, I spoke those words and now they poison me:
What will the deed do then?
Advancement? True, as high as shame can pitch.
For treasure, who e'er knew a harlot rich?
Or could build, by the purchase of her sin,
An hospital to keep their bastards in?
The duke's son? O, when women are young
Courtiers they are sure to be old beggars:
To know the miseries most harlots taste
Thou'ldst wish thyself unborn when thou art unchaste.

CASTIZA. O mother, let me twine about your neck
And kiss you till my soul melt on your lips:
I did but this to try you.

GRATIANA. O speak truth!

---

123 *kind*: either 'be kind' or 'kind daughter'.
128 *infect*: infected.
132 *held*: see Textual note, p. 196.
133 'I am now again your real mother.'
140 *purchase*: profit.
141 *hospital*: orphanage.

CASTIZA. Indeed, I did not, for no tongue has force to
alter me from honest.
If maidens would, men's words could have no power;
A virgin honour is a crystal tower,
Which, being weak, is guarded with good spirits;
Until she basely yields no ill inherits.
GRATIANA. O happy child! Faith and thy birth hath
saved me.
'Mongst thousand daughters happiest of all others
Buy thou a glass for maids and I for mothers.
Exeunt CASTIZA *and* GRATIANA.

ACT V

SCENE I

Enter VINDICE *and* HIPPOLITO. *They carry the corpse of the old duke, dressed in 'Piato's' disguise, and set it in place.*

VINDICE. So, so he leans well; take heed you wake him
not
Brother.
HIPPOLITO. I warrant you, my life for yours.
VINDICE. That's a good lay, for I must kill myself.
Brother, that's I, that sits for me: do you mark it.
And I must stand ready here to make away myself
yonder. I must sit to be killed and stand to kill myself.
I could vary it not so little as thrice over again; 't'as
some eight returns, like Michaelmas Term.
HIPPOLITO. That's enow, o'conscience.
VINDICE. But, sirrah, does the duke's son come single?

---

149 *I did not*: elliptical = I did not mean what I said about prostituting myself.
151 *would*: i.e. would be virtuous.
154 *inherits*: lives there, is present.
157 *Buy*: see Textual note, p. 196.
glass: mirror (as a model).
3 *lay*: bet.
8 *eight returns*: Michaelmas Term lasted eight weeks; a return was a report confirming a writ or Court Order.

HIPPOLITO. No, there's the hell on't, his faith's too feeble to go alone: he brings flesh-flies after him that will buzz against suppertime and hum for his coming out.

VINDICE. Ah, the fly-flop of vengeance beat 'em to pieces! Here was the sweetest occasion, the fittest hour, to have made my revenge familiar with him, show him the body of the duke his father and how quaintly he died, like a politician in hugger-mugger, made no man acquainted with it, and in catastrophe slain him over his father's breast, and – O, I'm mad to lose such a sweet opportunity.

HIPPOLITO. Nay, push, prithee be content. There's no remedy present. May not hereafter times open as fair faces as this?

VINDICE. They may, if they can paint so well.

HIPPOLITO. Come now, to avoid all suspicion let's forsake this room and be going to meet the duke's son.

VINDICE. Content, I'm for any weather. Heart, step close – here he comes.

Enter LUSSURIOSO.

HIPPOLITO. My honoured lord.
LUSSURIOSO. O me! You both present?

VINDICE. E'en newly arrived, my lord, just as your lordship entered now. About this place we had notice given he should be, but in some loathsome plight or other.

HIPPOLITO. Came your honour private?
LUSSURIOSO. Private enough for this; only a few
Attend my coming out.
VINDICE. (*aside*) Death rot those few.
LUSSURIOSO. Stay, yonder's the slave.
VINDICE. Mass, there's the slave, indeed, my lord.
(*Aside*) 'Tis a good child: he calls his father slave.
LUSSURIOSO. Ay, that's the villain, the damned villain. Softly,
Tread easy.

---

12 *flesh-flies*: blow-flies and hence parasites, hangers-on.
14 *fly-flop*: fly-swatter.
18 *politician*: here, secret intriguer.
in hugger-mugger: in secret.
19 *catastrophe*: a reference to the final movement of a tragedy.
23 *open*: provide.

VINDICE. Pooh, I warrant you, my lord;
We'll stifle in our breaths.
LUSSURIOSO. That will do well.
Base rogue, thou sleep'st thy last – (*Aside*) 'Tis policy
To have him killed in sleep, for if he waked
He would betray all to them.
VINDICE. But, my lord . . .
LUSSURIOSO. Ha, what say'st?
VINDICE. Shall we kill him now he's drunk?
LUSSURIOSO. Ay, best of all.
VINDICE. Why then he will ne'er live
To be sober.
LUSSURIOSO. No matter, let him reel to hell.
VINDICE. But being so full of liquor, I fear he will
Put out all the fire . . .
LUSSURIOSO. Thou art a mad beast.
VINDICE. (*aside*) . . . and leave none to warm your lordship's golls withall. –
For he that dies drunk falls into hellfire
Like a bucket o'water, qush, qush.
LUSSURIOSO. Come,
Be ready, nake your swords, think of your wrongs:
This slave has injured you.
VINDICE. Troth, so he has. –
(*Aside*) And he has paid well for't.
LUSSURIOSO. Meet with him now.
VINDICE. You'll bear us out, my lord?
LUSSURIOSO. Pooh, am I a lord for nothing, think you?
Quickly now.
VINDICE. Sa, sa, thump.
Stabs the corpse.
There he lies.
LUSSURIOSO. Nimbly done. Ha! O villains, murderers,
'Tis the old duke, my father.
VINDICE. That's a jest.
LUSSURIOSO. What? Stiff and cold already?
O pardon me to call you from your names,
'Tis none of your deed. That villain Piato,
Whom you thought now to kill, has murdered him

51 *golls*: hands.
54 *nake*: unsheath.
64 *to . . . names*: for using the wrong terms to describe you.

And left him thus disguised.

HIPPOLITO. And not unlikely.

VINDICE. O rascal! Was he not ashamed
To put the duke into a greasy doublet?

LUSSURIOSO. He has been cold and stiff who knows how long?

VINDICE. (*aside*) Marry, that do I.

LUSSURIOSO. No words, I pray, of anything intended.

VINDICE. O my lord.

HIPPOLITO. I would fain have your lordship think that we have small reason to prate.

LUSSURIOSO. Faith, thou say'st true. I'll forthwith send to court,
For all the nobles, bastard, duchess, all,
How here by miracle we found him dead
And in his raiment that foul villain fled.

VINDICE. That will be the best way, my lord, to clear us all; let's cast about to be clear.

LUSSURIOSO. Ho, Nencio, Sordido, and the rest!

Enter his attendants.

FIRST SERVANT. My lord?

LUSSURIOSO. Be witnesses of a strange spectacle.
Choosing for private conference that sad room
We found the duke my father 'gealed in blood.

FIRST SERVANT. My lord the duke! Run, hie thee, Nencio,
Startle the court by signifying so much.

Exit NENCIO.

VINDICE. (*aside*) Thus much by wit a deep revenger can:
When murder's known, to be the clearest man.
We're farthest off and with as bold an eye
Survey his body as the standers-by.

LUSSURIOSO. My royal father, too basely let blood
By a malevolent slave!

HIPPOLITO. (*to Vindice*) Hark,
He calls thee slave again.

VINDICE. H'as lost: he may.

---

74 *prate*: gossip.
86 *'gealed*: congealed.
88 *Thus*: see Textual note, p. 196.
89 *clearest*: seemingly innocent.
90 *farthest*: see Textual note, p. 196.

LUSSURIOSO. O sight! Look hither, see, his lips are gnawn
With poison.
VINDICE. How, his lips? By th'mass, they be!
LUSSURIOSO. O villain! O rogue! O slave! O rascal!
HIPPOLITO. (*aside*) O good deceit: he quits him with like terms.
FIRST VOICE. (*from within*) Where?
SECOND VOICE. (*from within*) Which way?

Enter AMBITIOSO *and* SUPERVACUO, *with nobles and gentlemen.*

AMBITIOSO. Over what roof hangs this prodigious comet
In deadly fire?
LUSSURIOSO. Behold, behold, my lords.
The duke my father's murdered, by a vassal that owes
this habit, and here left disguised.

Enter DUCHESS *and* SPURIO.

DUCHESS. My lord and husband!
SECOND NOBLE. Reverend majesty!
FIRST NOBLE. I have seen these clothes often attending on him.
VINDICE. (*aside*) That nobleman has been i'th'country, for he does not lie!
SUPERVACUO. (*to Ambitioso*) Learn of our mother – let's dissemble too.
I am glad he's vanished: so I hope are you.
AMBITIOSO. Ay, you may take my word for't.
SPURIO. Old dad dead?
(*Aside*) I, one of his cast sins, will send the fates
Most hearty commendations by his own son:
I'll tug in the new stream till strength be done.
LUSSURIOSO. Where be those two that did affirm to us
My lord the duke was privately rid forth?
FIRST GENTLEMAN. O pardon us, my lords. He gave that charge
Upon our lives, if he were missed at court,
To answer so: he rode not anywhere.

---

96 See Textual note, p. 196.
103 *owes*: owns.
111 *I*: see Textual note, p. 196.
cast: rejected.
116 *charge*: order.

We left him private with that fellow here.
VINDICE. (*aside*) Confirmed.
LUSSURIOSO. O heavens, that false charge was his death.
Impudent beggars! Durst you to our face
Maintain such a false answer? Bear him straight
To execution.
FIRST GENTLEMAN. My lord!
LUSSURIOSO. Urge me no more.
In this, the excuse may be called half the murder.
VINDICE. You've sentenced well.
LUSSURIOSO. Away, see it be done.
Exit first gentleman, guarded.
VINDICE. (*aside*) Could you not stick? See what confession doth.
Who would not lie when men are hanged for truth?
HIPPOLITO. (*to Vindice*) Brother, how happy is our vengeance.
VINDICE. Why, it hits
Past the apprehension of indifferent wits.
LUSSURIOSO. My lord, let post horse be sent into all
Places to entrap the villain.
VINDICE. (*aside*) Post horse, ha, ha!
FIRST NOBLE. My lord, we're something bold to know our duty.
Your father's accidently departed:
The titles that were due to him meet you.
LUSSURIOSO. Meet me? I'm not at leisure, my good lord;
I've many griefs to dispatch out o'th'way.
(*Aside*) Welcome, sweet titles. – Talk to me, my lords,
Of sepulchres and mighty emperors' bones:
That's thought for me.
VINDICE. (*aside*) So one may see by this
How foreign markets go:
Courtiers have feet o'th'nines and tongues o'th' twelves:
They flatter dukes and dukes flatter themselves.

---

125 s.d. See Textual note, p. 196.
126 *Could . . . stick*: Couldn't you keep quiet, or tell some story other than the truth?
141 Courtiers' tongues are three sizes larger than their feet.

SECOND NOBLE. My lord, it is your shine must comfort
us.
LUSSURIOSO. Alas, I shine in tears, like the sun in April.
FIRST NOBLE. You're now my lord's grace.
LUSSURIOSO. My lord's grace!
I perceive you'll have it so.
FIRST NOBLE. 'Tis but your own.
LUSSURIOSO. Then, heavens, give me grace to be so!
VINDICE. (*aside*) He prays well for himself.
SECOND NOBLE. (*to the duchess*) Madam, all sorrows
Must run their circles into joys. No doubt but time
Will make the murderer bring forth himself.
VINDICE. (*aside*) He were an ass then, i'faith.
FIRST NOBLE. In the mean season,
Let us bethink the latest funeral honours
Due to the duke's cold body; and, withall,
Calling to memory our new happiness,
Spread in his royal son. Lords, gentlemen,
Prepare for revels.
VINDICE. (*aside*) Revels!
SECOND NOBLE. Time hath several falls:
Griefs lift up joys, feasts put down funerals.
LUSSURIOSO. Come then, my lords, my favours to you all.
(*Aside*) The duchess is suspected foully bent:
I'll begin dukedom with her banishment.
Exeunt LUSSURIOSO, DUCHESS *and nobles.*
HIPPOLITO. (*to Vindice*) Revels!
VINDICE. Ay, that's the word; we are firm yet;
Strike one strain more and then we crown our wit.
Exeunt VINDICE *and* HIPPOLITO.
SPURIO. (*aside*) Well, have at the fairest mark –
So said the duke when he begot me –
And if I miss his heart or near about,
Then have at any; a bastard scorns to be out.
Exit SPURIO.

---

151 *mean season*: interim.
156 *falls*: falls are veils: Ross glosses the line, 'Time has several costumes, changes of shape.'
161 *firm*: safe.
162 *Strike . . . more*: play one more piece of music = play one more trick.
163 *mark*: target.

SUPERVACUO. Not'st thou that Spurio, brother?
AMBITIOSO. Yes, I note him to our shame.
SUPERVACUO. He shall not live; his hair shall not grow much longer. In this time of revels tricks may be set afoot. See'st thou yon new moon? It shall outlive the new duke by much: this hand shall dispossess him – then we're mighty.
A mask is treason's licence: that build upon;
'Tis murder's best face when a vizard's on.
Exit SUPERVACUO.
AMBITIOSO. Is't so? 'T's very good;
And do you think to be duke then, kind brother?
I'll see fair play: drop one and there lies tother.

SCENE II

Enter VINDICE *and* HIPPOLITO *with* PIERO *and other lords.*

VINDICE. My lords, be all of music;
Strike old griefs into other countries
That flow in too much milk and have faint livers,
Not daring to stab home their discontents.
Let our hid flames break out, as fire, as lightning,
To blast this villainous dukedom vexed with sin:
Wind up your souls to their full height again.
PIERO. How?
FIRST LORD. Which way?
THIRD LORD. Any way; our wrongs are such
We cannot justly be revenged too much.
VINDICE. You shall have all enough. Revels are toward,
And those few nobles that have long suppressed you
Are busied to the furnishing of a masque,
And do affect to make a pleasant tale on't.
The masquing suits are fashioning – now comes in
That which must glad us all: we to take pattern
Of all those suits, the colour, trimming, fashion,
E'en to an undistinguished hair almost.

---

3 *milk*: i.e. mildness, effeminacy.
faint livers: i.e. are cowardly (the liver being, in Elizabethan physiology, the home of strong emotion).
7 *Wind up*: lift, draw up (the image is probably musical – see l. 1 – suggesting the tightening of strings).
13 *affect*: endeavour, propose.

Then, ent'ring first, observing the true form,
Within a strain or two we shall find leisure
To steal our swords out handsomely,
And when they think their pleasure sweet and good,
In midst of all their joys they shall sigh blood.

PIERO. Weightily, effectually!

THIRD LORD. Before the tother masquers come . . .

VINDICE. We're gone, all done and past.

PIERO. But how for the duke's guard?

VINDICE. Let that alone;
By one and one their strengths shall be drunk down.

HIPPOLITO. There are five hundred gentlemen in the action
That will apply themselves and not stand idle.

PIERO. O, let us hug your bosoms!

VINDICE. Come, my lords,
Prepare for deeds: let other times have words.

Exeunt all.

SCENE III

In a dumb show the possessing of the young duke, with all his nobles; then sounding music. A furnished table is brought forth; then enters the duke and his nobles to the banquet. A blazing star appeareth.

FIRST NOBLE. Many harmonious hours and choicest pleasures
Fill up the royal numbers of your years.

LUSSURIOSO. My lords, we're pleased to thank you, though we know
'Tis but your duty now to wish it so.

SECOND NOBLE. That shine makes us all happy.

THIRD NOBLE. (*aside*) His grace frowns.

SECOND NOBLE. (*aside*) Yet we must say he smiles.

FIRST NOBLE. (*aside*) I think we must.

LUSSURIOSO. (*aside*) That foul, incontinent duchess we have banished;

---

18 *the true form*: i.e. the exact pattern of the proposed masque.
23 *effectually*: likely to be effective.
V.iii. s.d. *possessing*: putting in possession; formal installation.
A blazing star: see Additional note, p. 198.
5 *shine*: i.e. the graciousness of the new duke (which is conventionally compared with the shining of the sun).

The bastard shall not live. After these revels
I'll begin strange ones: he and the stepsons
Shall pay their lives for the first subsidies.
We must not frown so soon, else 'tad been now.

FIRST NOBLE. My gracious lord, please you prepare for pleasure,
The masque is not far off.

LUSSURIOSO. We are for pleasure –
(*To the star*) Beshrew thee, what art thou? Mad'st me start!
Thou hast committed treason. – A blazing star!

FIRST NOBLE. A blazing star, O where, my lord?

LUSSURIOSO. Spy out.

SECOND NOBLE. See, see, my lords, a wondrous-dreadful one!

LUSSURIOSO. I am not pleased at that ill-knotted fire,
That bushing, flaring star. Am I not duke?
It should not quake me now: had it appeared
Before it, I might then have justly feared.
But yet they say, whom art and learning weds,
When stars wear locks they threaten great men's heads.
Is it so? You are read, my lords.

FIRST NOBLE. May it please your grace.
It shows great anger.

LUSSURIOSO. That does not please our grace.

SECOND NOBLE. Yet here's the comfort, my lord: many times,
When it seems most, it threatens farthest off.

LUSSURIOSO. Faith, and I think so too.

FIRST NOBLE. Beside, my lord,
You're gracefully established, with the loves
Of all your subjects; and for natural death,
I hope it will be threescore years a-coming.

LUSSURIOSO. True. No more but threescore years?

FIRST NOBLE. Fourscore, I hope, my lord.

SECOND NOBLE. And fivescore, I.

---

10 *subsidies*: i.e. as the first 'payments' to the new duke (a subsidy is basically a fiscal grant given to a monarch, usually by Parliament).

19 *bushing*: growing thick.

21 *it*: i.e. before I became duke.

27 *seems most*: seems nearest.

THIRD NOBLE. But 'tis my hope, my lord, you shall ne'er die.

LUSSURIOSO. Give me thy hand, these others I rebuke;
He that hopes so is fittest for a duke.
Thou shalt sit next me. Take your places, lords,
We're ready now for sports; let 'em set on. –
You thing! We shall forget you quite anon.

THIRD NOBLE. I hear 'em coming, my lord.

Enter the masque of revengers; the two brothers and two lords more.

LUSSURIOSO. Ah, 'tis well.
Brothers and bastard, you dance next in hell.

The revengers dance; at the end steal out their swords and these four kill the four at the table, in their chairs. It thunders.

VINDICE. Mark, thunder!
Dost know thy cue, thou big-voiced crier?
Dukes' groans are thunder's watchwords.

HIPPOLITO. So, my lords, you have enough.

VINDICE. Come, let's away, no ling'ring.

HIPPOLITO. Follow!
(*To the lords*) Go!

Exeunt HIPPOLITO *and the two lords.*

VINDICE. No power is angry when the lustful die;
When thunder claps, heaven likes the tragedy.

Exit VINDICE.

Enter the other masque of intended murderers: AMBITIOSO, SUPERVACUO, SPURIO *and a fourth lord, coming in dancing.* LUSSURIOSO *recovers a little in voice and groans. He calls, 'A guard, treason', at which they all start out of their measure and, turning towards the table, they find them all to be murdered.*

LUSSURIOSO. O, O.

SPURIO. Whose groan was that?

---

39 *thing*: the star.

48 *claps . . . tragedy*: both words include their theatrical usage within their range of meaning.

48 s.d. This elaborate stage direction includes words and actions which are the material of ll. 49–50.

LUSSURIOSO. Treason, a guard.
AMBITIOSO. How now? All murdered?
SUPERVACUO. Murdered!
FOURTH LORD. And those his nobles!
AMBITIOSO. Here's a labour saved;
I thought to have sped him. 'Sblood, how came this?
SUPERVACUO. Then I proclaim myself; now I am duke.
AMBITIOSO. Thou duke? Brother, thou liest.
Kills SUPERVACUO.
SPURIO. Slave, so dost thou.
Kills AMBITIOSO.
FOURTH LORD. Base villain, hast thou slain my lord and master?
Kills SPURIO.

Enter VINDICE, HIPPOLITO *and the two lords.*

VINDICE. Pistols! Treason! Murder! Help! Guard my lord
The duke!

Enter ANTONIO *and the guard.*

HIPPOLITO. Lay hold upon this traitor!
The fourth lord is seized.
LUSSURIOSO. O.
VINDICE. Alas, the duke is murdered!
HIPPOLITO. And the nobles.
VINDICE. Surgeons, surgeons! (*Aside*) Heart, does he breathe so long?
ANTONIO. A piteous tragedy, able to wake
An old man's eyes bloodshot.
LUSSURIOSO. O.
VINDICE. Look to my lord
The duke. (*Aside*) A vengeance throttle him.
(*To fourth lord*) Confess, thou murd'rous and unhallowed man,
Didst thou kill all these?
FOURTH LORD. None but the bastard, I.
VINDICE. How came the duke slain, then?
FOURTH LORD. We found him so.
LUSSURIOSO. O villain.

---

52 *sped him*: killed him.
53 See Textual note, p. 196.
60 *wake*: see Textual note, p. 196.

VINDICE. Hark.
LUSSURIOSO. Those in the masque did murder us.
VINDICE. Law you now, sir.
O marble impudence! Will you confess now?
FOURTH LORD. 'Slud, 'tis all false!
ANTONIO. Away with that foul monster
Dipped in a prince's blood.
FOURTH LORD. Heart, 'tis a lie!
ANTONIO. Let him have bitter execution.

Exit guard with fourth lord.

VINDICE. (*Aside*) New marrow! No, I cannot be expressed.
– How fares my lord the duke?
LUSSURIOSO. Farewell to all;
He that climbs highest has the greatest fall.
My tongue is out of office.
VINDICE. Air, gentlemen, air!
(*Whispers to Lussurioso*) Now thou'lt not prate on't,
'twas Vindice murdered thee.
LUSSURIOSO. O.
VINDICE. Murdered thy father.
LUSSURIOSO. O.
VINDICE. And I am he.

LUSSURIOSO *dies.*

Tell nobody. – So, so, the duke's departed.
ANTONIO. It was a deadly hand that wounded him;
The rest, ambitious who should rule and sway
After his death, were so made all away.
VINDICE. My lord was unlikely.
HIPPOLITO. (*to Antonio*) Now the hope
Of Italy lies in your reverend years.
VINDICE. Your hair will make the silver age again,
When there was fewer but more honest men.
ANTONIO. The burden's weighty and will press age down:

---

67 *Law you*: merely an exclamation. ('Laws' as an exclamation continues to be used in English for a long time after this: see e.g. Trollope, *Can You Forgive Her?* (Penguin ed.) p. 863.)

72 *New marrow*: more pleasing food for his revenge.

83 *unlikely*: unpromising.

85 *silver age*: the second of the four ages of classical mythology – the silver age was inferior to the golden but, nonetheless, a time of goodness and harmony.

May I so rule that heaven may keep the crown.
VINDICE. The rape of your good lady has been 'quited
With death on death.
ANTONIO. Just is the law above.
But of all things it puts me most to wonder
How the old duke came murdered.
VINDICE. O, my lord.
ANTONIO. It was the strangeliest carried: I've not heard
Of the like.
HIPPOLITO. 'Twas all done for the best, my lord.
VINDICE. All for your grace's good.
We may be bold to speak it now.
'Twas somewhat witty carried, though we say it –
'Twas we two murdered him.
ANTONIO. You two?
VINDICE. None else, i'faith, my lord; nay 'twas well
managed.
ANTONIO. Lay hands upon those villains.
VINDICE *and* HIPPOLITO *are seized.*
VINDICE. How? On us?
ANTONIO. Bear 'em to speedy execution.
VINDICE. Heart! Was't not for your good, my lord?
ANTONIO. My good? Away with 'em. Such an old man
as he!
You, that would murder him, would murder me!
VINDICE. Is't come about?
HIPPOLITO. 'Sfoot, brother, you begun.
VINDICE. May we not set as well as the duke's son?
Thou hast no conscience: are we not revenged?
Is there one enemy left alive amongst those?
'Tis time to die when we are ourselves our foes.
When murd'rers shut deeds close this curse does seal
'em:
If none disclose 'em, they themselves reveal 'em!
This murder might have slept in tongueless brass,
But for ourselves, and the world died an ass.
Now I remember too, here was Piato

---

88 *May*: see Textual note, p. 196.
keep: protect.
89 *'quited*: requited, avenged.
104 See Additional note, p. 198.
106 *set*: die, punning on son = sun.
112 *brass*: as in memorial brass tablets.

Brought forth a knavish sentence once.
No doubt, said he, but time
Will make the murderer bring forth himself.
'Tis well he died; he was a witch.
And now, my lord, since we are in forever:
This work is ours, which else might have been slipped;
And if we list we could have nobles clipped
And go for less than beggars, but we hate
To bleed so cowardly. We have enough
I'faith, we're well: our mother turned, our sister true,
We die after a nest of dukes – adieu.

Exeunt VINDICE *and* HIPPOLITO *guarded.*

ANTONIO. How subtly was that murder 'closed! Bear up
Those tragic bodies; 'tis a heavy season:
Pray heaven their blood may wash away all treason.

Finis.

---

115 *sentence*: pithy saying.
118 *a witch*: because he possessed prophetic powers.
121 *nobles clipped*: nobles = (i) noblemen, (ii) gold coins; clipped = (i) mutilated, perhaps executed, (ii) damaged these coins by trimming their edges.

THE ATHEISTS TRAGEDIE:

OR

The honest Man's Reuenge.

As in diuers places it hath often beene Acted.

WRITTEN

By *Cyril Tourneur.*

AT LONDON,

Printed for *Iohn Stepney*, and *Richard Redmere*, and are to be sold at their Shops at the West end of Paules.

1611.

Title-page of the 1611 Quarto of *The Atheist's Tragedy*, reproduced by permission of the Bodleian Library.

INTRODUCTORY NOTE

Sources

As for *The Revenger's Tragedy*, there is no known full source for *The Atheist's Tragedy* and the only incident in the play for which a source has been suggested, to my knowledge, is that in which Levidulcia manages to get Fresco out of her bedchamber. Langbaine, as early as 1691, suggested that this may have its source in Boccaccio's *Decameron* (seventh day, sixth tale) and Boccaccio's story is certainly close to the incident in Tourneur's play, but Foakes[1] has shown that the dramatist could have found the story in any of several other places. Eleanor Prosser's comments on Samuel Brandon's closet play *Virtuous Octavia* suggest to me that this play prefigures Tourneur's in several respects, specifically in Octavia's refusal to take revenge and her insistence on leaving the matter to the gods;[2] but I know of no evidence to suggest that Tourneur knew Brandon's work. The only other piece of possible source material is *The Commentaries of Sir Francis Vere* (published 1657); Tourneur may have seen this in manuscript and remembered it when he wrote his account of the siege of Ostend in which Charlemont, according to Borachio, died. But, as Foakes points out (ed. cit., p. xxxii) Tourneur was probably at the siege himself and there are few signs that Vere's account has verbally affected Tourneur.

There are other influences on *The Atheist's Tragedy*. Higgins[3] has shown a Calvinistic streak in the play's morality, while several critics have pointed to the probable effect of other plays on Tourneur. In a general way the figure of Levidulcia seems to owe a debt to Jacobean comedy (to Marston's *Dutch Courtesan*, for example), while, as Jenkins has suggested,[4] the opening and closing scenes may draw on *Hoffman* and *Antonio's Revenge* respectively. Jenkins also sees a link between Charlemont and Chapman's *Revenge of Bussy* (IV.i) and Ornstein (*The Moral Vision of Jacobean Tragedy*, p. 121) claims that Tourneur 'borrows and transforms the graveyard themes of *Hamlet*', and that he draws on *King Lear* for the presentation of 'the atheist's disillusionment with nature'.

Thus *The Atheist's Tragedy* is, like *The Revenger's Tragedy*, synthetic. But there is, I think, an important difference, for whereas the dramatist of the latter play is able to unify his material into a coherent and individualised whole, and has not

1 *The Revenger's Tragedy*, ed. R.A. Foakes (London: Methuen, 1966), p. xxif.
2 *Hamlet and Revenge* (Stanford University Press, 1971), p. 22.
3 'The influence of Calvinist thought on Tourneur's *Atheist's Tragedy*', *R.E.S.* XIX, 1943.
4 'Cyril Tourneur', *R.E.S.* XVII, 1941.

been dominated by the influences bearing on him, Tourneur fails to achieve this coherence and freedom in *The Atheist's Tragedy*, as one sees most obviously if one compares *Hamlet* and *Lear* with his use of these plays.

Stage-history

Apart from the rather unconvincing statement quoted earlier from the title-page of the first edition there is no stage-history of this play. I know of no revivals of it (in fact, a 'revival' might well be the premiѐre!), and it is difficult to imagine how the play could work on the modern stage without achieving the opposite of what seems to be Tourneur's intention.

A note on editions

The Atheist's Tragedy suffered from the attentions of Collins and Symonds in much the same way as *The Revenger's Tragedy* did. Since it is clearly the inferior play, this damage is, on one level, less serious, but, on the other hand, the facts that it is inferior and that it makes less immediate appeal to a modern reader mean that a good modern edition is needed in order that a reader can be helped to understand the sort of play this is. Broadly speaking, Irving Ribner's edition (Revels Plays, 1964) fulfils this need: the modernised text is sound, the annotation full, and the introduction provides both information and a brave critical account of the play. For anyone who wants to look at the first edition there is an inexpensive facsimile produced by the Scolar Press (1969).

DRAMATIS PERSONAE

MONTFERRERS, a baron
BELFOREST, a baron
D'AMVILLE, brother to Montferrers
LEVIDULCIA, Lady to Belforest
CASTABELLA, daughter to Belforest
CHARLEMONT, son to Montferrers
ROUSARD, elder son to D'Amville
SEBASTIAN, younger son to D'Amville
LANGUEBEAU SNUFF, a Puritan and chaplain to Belforest
BORACHIO, D'Amville's instrument
CATAPLASMA, a maker of periwigs and attires
SOQUETTE, a seeming gentlewoman to Cataplasma
FRESCO, a servant to Cataplasma
Other servants
Sergeant in war
Soldiers
Watchmen
Officers
Doctor
Judges
Prison keeper
Executioner

D'Amville	French 'D'Ame' and English 'vile' – hence 'evil-spirited'
Levidulcia	light and sweet
Castabella	chaste and beautiful
Languebeau	beautiful tongue ('smooth talking')
Borachio	drunkard
Cataplasma	poultice
Soquette	Ribner suggests from Italian 'soqquadrare' (to cause confusion)
Fresco	fresh

THE ATHEIST'S TRAGEDY

ACT I

SCENE I

Enter D'AMVILLE *and* BORACHIO *attended.*

D'AMVILLE. I saw my nephew Charlemont but now
Part from his father. Tell him I desire
To speak with him.

Exit servant.

Borachio, thou art read
In nature and her large philosophy.
Observ'st thou not the very self-same course
Of revolution both in man and beast?

BORACHIO. The same. For birth, growth, state, decay and death:
Only, a man's beholding to his nature
For th' better composition o' the two.

D'AMVILLE. But where that favour of his nature is
Not full and free you see a man becomes
A fool, as little-knowing as a beast.

BORACHIO. That shows there's nothing in a man above
His nature: if there were, consid'ring 'tis
His being's excellency, 'twould not yield
To nature's weakness.

D'AMVILLE. Then if death casts up
Our total sum of joy and happiness
Let me have all my senses feasted in
Th' abundant fullness of delight at once,
And with a sweet insensible increase
Of pleasing surfeit melt into my dust.

BORACHIO. That revolution is too short methinks.
If this life comprehends our happiness
How foolish to desire to die so soon?
And if our time runs home unto the length
Of nature, how improvident it were

---

7 *state*: worldly situation (here with associations of maturity).
9 *composition*: union.
16 *nature's weakness*: i.e. death.
casts up: adds up, summarises.
23 *comprehends*: sums up, includes all.
25–6 *time . . . nature*: if we live our natural span of life.

To spend our substance on a minute's pleasure
And after live an age in misery!
D'AMVILLE. So thou conclud'st that pleasure only flows
Upon the stream of riches?
BORACHIO. Wealth is lord
Of all felicity.
D'AMVILLE. 'Tis oracle,
For what's a man that's honest without wealth?
BORACHIO. Both miserable and contemptible.
D'AMVILLE. He's worse, Borachio. For if charity
Be an essential part of honesty,
And should be practised first upon ourselves –
Which must be granted – then your honest man
That's poor is most dishonest, for he is
Uncharitable to the man whom he
Should most respect. But what doth this touch me
That seem to have enough? Thanks industry
'Tis true. Had not my body spread itself
Into posterity perhaps I should
Desire no more increase of substance than
Would hold proportion with mine own dimensions.
Yet even in that sufficiency of state
A man has reason to provide and add:
For what is he hath such a present eye
And so prepared a strength, that can foresee
And fortify his substance and himself
Against those accidents the least whereof
May rob him of an age's husbandry?
And, for my children, they are as near to me
As branches to the tree whereon they grow,
And may as numerously be multiplied.
As they increase, so should my providence,
For from my substance they receive the sap
Whereby they live and flourish.
BORACHIO. Sir, enough,
I understand the mark whereat you aim.

Enter CHARLEMONT.

---

40 *respect*: take account of.
41 *industry*: see Textual note, p. 196.
45 'Would be in proportion to my own needs'.
46 *state*: see above l. 7.
56 *providence*: provision (for them).

D'AMVILLE. Silence, w'are interrupted. Charlemont!
CHARLEMONT. Good morrow, uncle.
D'AMVILLE. Noble Charlemont,
Good morrow. Is not this the honoured day
You purposed to set forward to the war?
CHARLEMONT. My inclination did intend it so.
D'AMVILLE. And not your resolution?
CHARLEMONT. Yes, my lord,
Had not my father contradicted it.
D'AMVILLE. O noble war! Thou first original
Of all man's honour. How dejectedly
The baser spirit of our present time
Hath cast itself below the ancient worth
Of our forefathers, from whose noble deeds
Ignobly we derive our pedigrees!
CHARLEMONT. Sir, tax not me for his unwillingness.
By the command of his authority
My disposition's forced against itself.
D'AMVILLE. Nephew, you are the honour of our blood.
The troop of gentry, whose inferior worth
Should second your example, are become
Your leaders, and the scorn of their discourse
Turns smiling back upon your backwardness.
CHARLEMONT. You need not urge my spirit by disgrace;
'Tis free enough. My father hinders it.
To curb me he denies me maintenance
To put me in the habit of my rank.
Unbind me from that strong necessity
And call me coward if I stay behind.
D'AMVILLE. For want of means? Borachio, where's the gold?
I'd disinherit my posterity
To purchase honour. 'Tis an interest
I prize above the principal of wealth.
I'm glad I had th'occasion to make known
How readily my substance shall unlock
Itself to serve you. Here's a thousand crowns.
CHARLEMONT. My worthy uncle, in exchange for this
I leave my bond. So I am doubly bound:

---

67 *first original*: origin.
84 *habit*: equipment.
90 *principal*: capital, with a pun on 'principle'.

By that for the repayment of this gold,
And by this gold to satisfy your love.
D'AMVILLE. Sir, 'tis a witness only of my love,
And love doth always satisfy itself.
Now to your father; labour his consent.
My importunity shall second yours.
We will obtain it.
CHARLEMONT. If entreaty fail,
The force of reputation shall prevail. *Exit.*
D'AMVILLE. Go call my sons that they may take their leaves
Of noble Charlemont.
Exit servant.
Now my Borachio!
BORACHIO. The substance of our former argument
Was wealth.
D'AMVILLE. The question how to compass it.
BORACHIO. Young Charlemont is going to the wars.
D'AMVILLE. O, thou begin'st to take me.
BORACHIO. Mark me then.
Methinks the pregnant wit of man might make
The happy absence of this Charlemont
A subject for commodious providence.
He has a wealthy father, ready ev'n
To drop into his grave. And no man's power,
When Charlemont is gone, can interpose
'Twixt you and him.
D'AMVILLE. Th'ast apprehended both
My meaning and my love. Now let thy trust,
For undertaking and for secrecy,
Hold measure with thy amplitude of wit,
And thy reward shall parallel thy worth.
BORACHIO. My resolution has already bound
Me to your service.
D'AMVILLE. And my heart to thee.

Enter ROUSARD *and* SEBASTIAN.

Here are my sons:
There's my eternity. My life in them

---

107 *compass*: achieve.
109 *take*: understand.
112 *commodious providence*: large-scale material gain.

And their succession shall for ever live,
And in my reason dwells the providence
To add to life as much of happiness.
Let all men lose, so I increase my gain
I have no feeling of another's pain.

Exeunt.

SCENE II

Enter old MONTFERRERS *and* CHARLEMONT.

MONTFERRERS. I prithee let this current of my tears
Divert thy inclination from the war,
For of my children thou art only left
To promise a succession to my house,
And all the honour thou canst get by arms
Will give but vain addition to thy name,
Since from thy ancestors thou dost derive
A dignity sufficient and as great
As thou hast substance to maintain and bear.
I prithee stay at home.

CHARLEMONT. My noble father,
The weakest sigh you breathe hath power to turn
My strongest purpose, and your softest tear
To melt my resolution to as soft
Obedience. But my affection to the war
Is as hereditary as my blood
To every life of all my ancestry.
Your predecessors were your precedents
And you are my example. Shall I serve
For nothing but a vain parenthesis
I'th'honoured story of your family?
Or hang but like an empty scutcheon
Between the trophies of my predecessors
And the rich arms of my posterity?
There's not a Frenchman of good blood and youth

5f. For the background to this debate about honour see Ruth Kelso, *The Doctrine of The English Gentleman in the Sixteenth Century* (University of Illinois Press, 1929).

14–16 'My desire to go to war is as much an inheritance from my ancestors as is my blood.'

19 *parenthesis*: interval, gap.

21 *empty scutcheon*: blank shield.

But either out of spirit or example
Is turned a soldier. Only Charlemont
Must be reputed that same heartless thing
That cowards will be bold to play upon.

Enter D'AMVILLE, ROUSARD *and* SEBASTIAN.

D'AMVILLE. Good morrow, my lord.
MONTFERRERS. Morrow, good brother.
CHARLEMONT. Good morrow, uncle.
D'AMVILLE. Morrow, kind nephew.
What, ha'you washed your eyes wi'tears this morning?
(*To Montferrers*) Come, by my soul, his purpose does deserve
Your free consent. Your tenderness dissuades him.
What to the father of a gentleman
Should be more tender than the maintenance
And the increase of honour to his house?
My lord, here are my boys. I should be proud
That either this were able or that inclined
To be my nephew's brave competitor.
MONTFERRERS. Your importunities have overcome.
Pray God my forced grant prove not ominous.
D'AMVILLE. (*to Charlemont*) We have obtained it. (*To Montferrers*) Ominous? In what?
It cannot be in anything but death,
And I am of a confident belief
That ev'n the time, place, manner of our deaths
Do follow Fate with that necessity
That makes us sure to die. And in a thing
Ordained so certainly unalterable
What can the use of providence prevail?

Enter BELFOREST, LEVIDULCIA, CASTABELLA, *attended.*

BELFOREST. Morrow, my lord Montferrers, lord D'Amville,
Good morrow, gentlemen; cousin Charlemont
Kindly good morrow. Troth, I was afeared
I should ha'come too late to tell you that
I wish your undertakings a success
That may deserve the measure of their worth.

---

35 *tender*: precious.

CHARLEMONT. My lord, my duty would not let me go
Without receiving your commandéments.
BELFOREST. Accompliments are more for ornament
Than use. We should employ no time in them
But what our serious business will admit.
MONTFERRERS. Your favour had by his duty been prevented
If we had not withheld him in the way.
D'AMVILLE. He was a-coming to present his service.
But now no more. The cook invites to breakfast:
Wilt please your lordship enter? Noble lady?
Exeunt all except CHARLEMONT *and* CASTABELLA.
CHARLEMONT. My noble mistress, this accompliment
Is like an elegant and moving speech
Composed of many sweet, persuasive points
Which second one another with a fluent
Increase and confirmation of their force,
Reserving still the best until the last
To crown the strong impulsion of the rest
With a full conquest of the hearer's sense,
Because th'impression of the last we speak
Doth always longest and most constantly
Possess the entertainment of remembrance.
So all that now salute my taking leave
Have added numerously to the love
Wherewith I did receive their courtesy.
But you, dear mistress, being the last and best
That speaks my farewell, like th'imperious close
Of a most sweet oration, wholly have
Possessed my liking, and shall ever live
Within the soul of my true memory.
So, mistress, with this kiss I take my leave.
CASTABELLA. My worthy servant, you mistake th'intent
Of kissing: 'twas not meant to separate
A pair of lovers, but to be the seal
Of love, importing by the joining of
Our mutual and incorporated breaths

---

57 *commandéments*: see Textual note, p. 196.
58 *Accompliments*: here 'compliments'.
61 *prevented*: anticipated.
63 *a-coming*: see Textual note, p. 196.
72 *impulsion*: forward movement.

That we should breathe but one contracted life.
Or stay at home or let me go with you.
CHARLEMONT. My Castabella, for myself to stay
Or you to go would either tax my youth
With a dishonourable weakness or
Your loving purpose with immodesty.

Enter LANGUEBEAU SNUFF.

And for the satisfaction of your love
Here comes a man whose knowledge I have made
A witness to the contract of our vows,
Which my return by marriage shall confirm.
LANGUEBEAU. I salute you both with the spirit of copulation. I am already informed of your matrimonial purposes and will be a testimony to the integrity of your promises.
CASTABELLA. O the sad trouble of my fearful soul!
My faithful servant, did you never hear
That when a certain great man went to the war
The lovely face of heaven was masked with sorrow,
The sighing winds did move the breast of earth,
The heavy clouds hung down their mourning heads
And wept sad showers the day that he went hence,
As if that day presaged some ill success
That fatally should kill his happiness –
And so it came to pass. Methinks my eyes
(Sweet heaven forbid!) are like those weeping clouds,
And as their showers presaged so do my tears.
Some sad event will follow my sad fears.
CHARLEMONT. Fie, superstitious, is it bad to kiss?
CASTABELLA. May all my fears hurt me no more than this.
They kiss.
LANGUEBEAU. Fie, fie, fie, these carnal kisses do stir up the concupiscences of the flesh.

---

91 *contracted*: (a) united, (b) betrothed, engaged.
94 *tax*: censure, blame.
101–4 After making the point that Languebeau is throughout given jargon associated with Puritans, Ribner refers to W.P. Holden *Anti-Puritan Satire 1572–1642* (New Haven, 1954), pp. 107–8.
106f. Although this is sometimes taken as a reference to Sir Francis Vere, the lines are not specific enough to make this anything more than conjecture.

Enter BELFOREST *and* LEVIDULCIA.

LEVIDULCIA. O, here's your daughter under her servant's lips.

CHARLEMONT. Madam, there is no cause you should mistrust
The kiss I gave; 'twas but a parting one.

LEVIDULCIA. A lusty blood! Now, by the lip of love,
Were I to choose, your joining one for me!

BELFOREST. Your father stays to bring you on the way.
Farewell. The great commander of the war
Prosper the course you undertake. Farewell.

CHARLEMONT. My lord I humbly take my leave. (*To Levidulcia*) Madam,
I kiss your hand. (*To Castabella*) And your sweet lip. Farewell.

Exeunt all except CHARLEMONT *and* LANGUEBEAU.

Her power to speak is perished in her tears.
Something within me would persuade my stay,
But reputation will not yield unto't.
Dear sir, you are the man whose honest trust
My confidence hath chosen for my friend.
I fear my absence will discomfort her.
You have the power and opportunity
To moderate her passion. Let her grief
Receive that friendship from you, and your love
Shall not repent itself of courtesy.

LANGUEBEAU. Sir, I want words and protestation to insinuate into your credit, but, in plainness and truth, I will qualify her grief with the spirit of consolation.

CHARLEMONT. Sir, I will take your friendship up at use;
And fear not that your profit shall be small –
Your int'rest shall exceed your principal.

Exit CHARLEMONT.

Enter D'AMVILLE *and* BORACHIO.

D'AMVILLE. Monsieur Languebeau, happily encountered. The honesty of your conversation makes me request

---

125–6 See Textual note, p. 196.

128 *great commander*: this may refer to God, Mars, or even Montferrers.

146 *use*: i.e. monetary interest.

150–1 *makes . . . familiarity*: makes me ask to know you better.

more interest in your familiarity.

LANGUEBEAU. If your lordship will be pleased to salute me without ceremony I shall be willing to exchange my service for your favour, but this worshipping kind of entertainment is a superstitious vanity: in plainness and truth I love it not.

D'AMVILLE. I embrace your disposition and desire to give you as liberal assurance of my love as my lord Belforest, your deserved favourer.

LANGUEBEAU. His lordship is pleased with my plainness and truth of conversation.

D'AMVILLE. It cannot displease him. In the behaviour of his noble daughter Castabella a man may read her worth and your instruction.

LANGUEBEAU. That gentlewoman is most sweetly modest, fair, honest, handsome, wise, well-born and rich.

D'AMVILLE. You have given me her picture in small.

LANGUEBEAU. She's like your diamond: a temptation in every man's eye, yet not yielding to any light impression herself.

D'AMVILLE. The praise is hers, but the comparison your own.

Gives him a ring.

LANGUEBEAU. You shall forgive me that, sir.

D'AMVILLE. I will not do so much at your request as – forgive you it. I will only give you it sir. By . . . you will make me swear.

LANGUEBEAU. O, by no means! Profane not your lips with the foulness of that sin. I will rather take it. To save your oath you shall lose your ring. Verily, my lord, my praise came short of her worth. She exceeds a jewel: this is but only for ornament – she both for ornament and use.

D'AMVILLE. Yet unprofitably kept without use. She deserves a worthy husband, sir. I have often wished a match between my elder son and her. The marriage would join the houses of Belforest and D'Amville into a noble alliance.

168–70 A diamond cannot easily be scratched or marked: so Castabella, as attractive as a diamond, cannot easily be marked by any wanton approach.

172 s.d. See Textual note, p. 196.

LANGUEBEAU. And the unity of families is a work of love and charity.

D'AMVILLE. And that work an employment well becoming the goodness of your disposition.

LANGUEBEAU. If your lordship please to impose it upon me I will carry it without any second end, the surest way to satisfy your wish.

D'AMVILLE. Most joyfully accepted – Rousard – Here are letters to my lord Belforest touching my desire to that purpose.

Enter ROUSARD, *sickly.*

Rousard, I send you a suitor to Castabella. To this gentleman's discretion I commit the managing of your suit. His good success shall be most thankful to your trust. Follow his instructions, he will be your leader.

LANGUEBEAU. In plainness and truth.

ROUSARD. My leader? Does your lordship think me too weak to give the onset myself?

LANGUEBEAU. I will only assist your proceedings.

ROUSARD. To say true, so I think you had need, for a sick man can hardly get a woman's good will without help.

LANGUEBEAU. (*aside*) Charlemont! Thy gratuity and my promises were both but words, and both, like words, shall vanish into air.
For thy poor empty hand I must be mute:
This gives me feeling of a better suit.

Exeunt LANGUEBEAU *and* ROUSARD.

D'AMVILLE. Borachio, didst precisely note this man?

BORACHIO. His own profession would report him pure.

D'AMVILLE. And seems to know if any benefit
Arises of religion after death.
Yet but compare's profession with his life,
They so directly contradict themselves
As if the end of his instructions were
But to divert the world from sin, that he
More easily might engross it to himself:

---

193 *second end*: other motive.
200–1 *good . . . trust*: his success will help you if you trust him.
209 *gratuity*: present, tip.
222 *engross*: collect.

By that I am confirmed an atheist.
Well, Charlemont is gone – and here thou see'st
His absence the foundation of my plot.

BORACHIO. He is the man whom Castabella loves.

D'AMVILLE. That was the reason I propounded him
Employment fixed upon a foreign place,
To draw his inclination out o'the way.

BORACHIO. 'Thas left the passage of our practice free.

D'AMVILLE. This Castabella is a wealthy heir,
And by her marriage with my elder son
My house is honoured and my state increased.
This work alone deserves my industry,
But if it prosper thou shalt see my brain
Make this but an induction to a point
So full of profitable policy
That it would make the soul of honesty
Ambitious to turn villain.

BORACHIO. I bespeak
Employment in't. I'll be an instrument
To grace performance with dexterity.

D'AMVILLE. Thou shalt. No man shall rob you of the honour.
Go presently and buy a crimson scarf
Like Charlemont's. Prepare thee a disguise
I'th'habit of a soldier hurt and lame,
And then be ready at the wedding feast,
Where thou shalt have employment in a work
Will please thy disposition.

BORACHIO. As I vowed,
Your instrument shall make your project proud.

D'AMVILLE. This marriage will bring wealth: if that succeed,
I will increase it though my brother bleed.

Exeunt.

---

227 *propounded*: proposed to.
236 *induction*: introduction.
237 *policy*: with, of course, Machiavellian overtones of sly dealings.

SCENE III

Enter CASTABELLA, *avoiding the importunity of* ROUSARD.

CASTABELLA. Nay, good sir, in troth if you knew how little it pleases me you would forbear it.

ROUSARD. I will not leave thee till th'ast entertained me for thy servant.

CASTABELLA. My servant? You are sick, you say. You would tax me of indiscretion to entertain one that is not able to do me service.

ROUSARD. The service of a gentlewoman consists most in chamber work and sick men are fittest for the chamber. I prithee give me a favour.

CASTABELLA. Methinks you have a very sweet favour of your own.

ROUSARD. I lack but your black eye.

CASTABELLA. If you go to buffets among the boys they'll give you one.

ROUSARD. Nay, if you grow bitter I'll dispraise your black eye. The grey-eyed morning makes the fairest day.

CASTABELLA. Now that you dissemble not I could be willing to give you a favour. What favour would you have?

ROUSARD. Any toy, any light thing.

CASTABELLA. Fie, will you be so uncivil to ask a light thing at a gentlewoman's hand?

ROUSARD. Wilt give me a bracelet o'thy hair then?

CASTABELLA. Do you want hair, sir?

ROUSARD. No, faith, I'll want no hair so long as I can have it for money.

CASTABELLA. What would you with my hair then?

---

4 *servant*: suitor.

7 *service*: here, as in l. 8, the word's meaning includes its sexual sense.

11 *favour*: appearance.

13 *black eye*: granted the tone of these exchanges the sexual sense (vagina) suggested by Ribner is quite likely.

21–2 *light*: Rousard's basic meaning is 'trivial', while Castabella gives the word the sense of 'wanton'.

24 *bracelet . . . hair*: as a love-token. The following remarks about lacking hair and having it worn off refer to loss of hair as a result of venereal disease.

ROUSARD. Wear it for thy sake, sweetheart.

CASTABELLA. Do you think I love to have my hair worn off?

ROUSARD. Come, you are so witty now and so sensible. *Kisses her.*

CASTABELLA. Tush, I would I wanted one o'my senses now.

ROUSARD. Bitter again? What's that? Smelling?

CASTABELLA. No, no, no. Why now y'are satisfied I hope. I have given you a favour.

ROUSARD. What favour? A kiss? I prithee give me another.

CASTABELLA. Show me that I gave you then.

ROUSARD. How should I show it?

CASTABELLA. You are unworthy of a favour if you will not bestow the keeping of it one minute.

ROUSARD. Well, in plain terms, dost love me? That's the purpose of my coming.

CASTABELLA. Love you? Yes, very well.

ROUSARD. Give me thy hand upon't.

CASTABELLA. Nay you mistake me. If I love you very well I must not love you now, for now you are not very well – y'are sick.

ROUSARD. This equivocation is for the jest now.

CASTABELLA. I speak't as 'tis now in fashion, in earnest. But I shall not be in quiet for you, I perceive, till I have given you a favour. Do you love me?

ROUSARD. With all my heart.

CASTABELLA. Then with all my heart I'll give you a jewel to hang in your ear. Hark ye – I can never love you. *Exit.*

ROUSARD. Call you this a jewel to hang in mine ear? 'Tis no light favour for I'll be sworn it comes somewhat heavily to me. Well, I will not leave her for all this. Methinks it animates a man to stand to it when a woman desires to be rid of him at the first sight. *Exit.*

---

32 *sensible*: sensitive.
53 *in quiet for*: in peace from.

SCENE IV

Enter BELFOREST *and* LANGUEBEAU SNUFF.

BELFOREST. I entertain the offer of this match
With purpose to confirm it presently.
I have already moved it to my daughter:
Her soft excuses savoured at the first
(Methought) but of a modest innocence
Of blood, whose unmoved stream was never drawn
Into the current of affection. But when I
Replied with more familiar arguments,
Thinking to make her apprehension bold,
Her modest blush fell to a pale dislike
And she refused it with such confidence
As if she had been prompted by a love
Inclining firmly to some other man,
And in that obstinacy she remains.

LANGUEBEAU. Verily that disobedience doth not become a child. It proceedeth from an unsanctified liberty. You will be accessory to your own dishonour if you suffer it.

BELFOREST. Your honest wisdom has advised me well.
Once more I'll move her by persuasive means.
If she resist, all mildness set apart,
I will make use of my authority.

LANGUEBEAU. And instantly, lest – fearing your constraint – her contrary affection teach her some device that may prevent you.

BELFOREST. To cut off every opportunity
Procrastination may assist her with
This instant night she shall be marrièd.

LANGUEBEAU. Best.

Enter CASTABELLA.

CASTABELLA. Please it your lordship, my mother attends
I'the gallery and desires your conference.

Exit BELFOREST.

This means I used to bring me to your ear.
Time cuts off circumstance; I must be brief.
To your integrity did Charlemont
Commit the contract of his love and mine,

---

8 *familiar*: intimate.
31 *desires your conference*: wishes to speak with you.

Which now so strong a hand seeks to divide
That if your grave advice assist me not
I shall be forced to violate my faith.

LANGUEBEAU. Since Charlemont's absence I have weighed his love with the spirit of consideration, and in sincerity I find it to be frivolous and vain. Withdraw your respect: his affection deserveth it not.

CASTABELLA. Good sir, I know your heart cannot profane
The holiness you make profession of
With such a vicious purpose as to break
The vow your own consent did help to make.

LANGUEBEAU. Can he deserve your love who, in neglect of your delightful conversation and in obstinate contempt of all your prayers and tears, absents himself so far from your sweet fellowship and with a purpose so contracted to that absence that you see he purchases your separation with the hazard of his blood and life, fearing to want pretence to part your companies? 'Tis rather hate that doth division move: love still desires the presence of his love. Verily he is not of the Family of Love.

CASTABELLA. O do not wrong him. 'Tis a generous mind
That led his disposition to the war,
For gentle love and noble courage are
So near allied that one begets another,
Or love is sister and courage is the brother.
Could I affect him better than before
His soldier's heart would make me love him more.

LANGUEBEAU. But, Castabella . . .

Enter LEVIDULCIA.

LEVIDULCIA. Tush, you mistake the way into a woman:
The passage lies not through her reason but her blood.
Exit LANGUEBEAU; CASTABELLA *about to follow.*
Nay stay! How wouldst thou call the child
That, being raised with cost and tenderness
To full ability of body and means,

47ff. See Textual note, p. 196.
51 *contracted*: firmly dedicated.
55–6 *Family of Love*: a religious sect founded *c.* 1540 in Holland and often attacked as advocating sexual laxity.
62 *affect*: love.

Denies relief unto the parents who
Bestowed that bringing up?
CASTABELLA. Unnatural.
LEVIDULCIA. Then Castabella is unnatural.
Nature, the loving mother of us all,
Brought forth a woman for her own relief,
By generation to revive her age:
Which, now thou hast ability and means
Presented, most unkindly dost deny.
CASTABELLA. Believe me, mother, I do love a man.
LEVIDULCIA. Prefer'st th'affection of an absent love
Before the sweet possession of a man?
The barren mind before the fruitful body
Where our creation has no reference
To man but in his body, being made
Only for generation, which (unless
Our children can be gotten by conceit)
Must from the body come? If reason were
Our counsellor we would neglect the work
Of generation for the prodigal
Expense it draws us to, of that which is
The wealth of life. Wise nature, therefore, hath
Reserved for an inducement to our sense
Our greatest pleasure in that greatest work,
Which, being offered thee, thy ignorance
Refuses for th'imaginary joy
Of an unsatisfied affection to
An absent man, whose blood once spent i'th'war,
Then he'll come home sick, lame and impotent,
And wed thee to a torment like the pain
Of Tantalus, continuing thy desire
With fruitless presentation of the thing
It loves, still moved and still unsatisfied.

Enter BELFOREST, D'AMVILLE, ROUSARD, SEBASTIAN, LANGUEBEAU *etc.*

---

77 *unkindly*: unnaturally.
85 *conceit*: imagination.
86–90 The reference is to the common idea that sexual intercourse shortened life.
99 *Tantalus*: in Hades Tantalus is tormented with food and drink that is eternally out of reach.

BELFOREST. Now, Levidulcia, hast thou yet prepared
My daughter's love to entertain this man,
Her husband here?
LEVIDULCIA. I'm but her mother-i'-law,
Yet if she were my very flesh and blood
I could advise no better for her good.
ROUSARD. Sweet wife! Thy joyful husband thus salutes
Thy cheek.
CASTABELLA. My husband? O, I am betrayed.
(*To Languebeau*) Dear friend of Charlemont, your purity
Professes a divine contempt o'the world;
O be not bribed by that you so neglect
In being the world's hated instrument
To bring a just neglect upon yourself.
Kneels from one to another.
(*To Belforest*) Dear father, let me but examine my
Affection. (*To D'Amville*) Sir, your prudent judgement can
Persuade your son that 'tis improvident
To marry one whose disposition he
Did ne'er observe. (*To Rousard*) Good sir, I may be of
A nature so unpleasing to your mind
Perhaps you'll curse the fatal hour wherein
You rashly married me.
D'AMVILLE. My lord Belforest,
I would not have her forced against her choice.
BELFOREST. Passion o'me, thou peevish girl. I charge
Thee by my blessing, and the authority
I have to claim thy obedience: marry him.
CASTABELLA. Now Charlemont! O my presaging tears!
This sad event hath followed my sad fears.
SEBASTIAN. A rape, a rape, a rape!
BELFOREST. How now?
D'AMVILLE. What's that?
SEBASTIAN. Why, what is't but a rape to force a wench to marry, since it forces her to lie with him she would not.

---

106 *her good*: see Textual note, p. 196.
114–15 *examine my Affection*: consider where my feelings lie.
129–31 See Textual note, p. 196.

LANGUEBEAU. Verily, his tongue is an unsanctified member.

SEBASTIAN. Verily, your gravity becomes your perished soul as hoary mouldiness does rotten fruit.

BELFOREST. Cousin, y'are both uncivil and profane.

D'AMVILLE. Thou disobedient villain, get thee out of my sight. Now by my soul I'll plague thee for this rudeness.

BELFOREST. Come, set forward to the church.

Exeunt: SEBASTIAN *remains.*

SEBASTIAN. And verify the proverb 'The nearer the church the further from God'. Poor wench. For thy sake may his ability die in his appetite, that thou be'st not troubled with him thou lovest not. May his appetite move thy desire to another man so he shall help to make himself cuckold. And let that man be one that he pays wages to, so thou shalt profit by him thou hatest. Let the chambers be matted, the hinges oiled, the curtain-rings silenced and the chamber-maid hold her peace at his own request that he may sleep the quieter. And in that sleep let him be soundly cuckolded. And when he knows it and seeks to sue a divorce let him have no other satisfaction than this: 'He lay by her and slept: the law will take no hold of her because he winked at it.'

Exit.

ACT II

SCENE I

Music, a banquet, in the night. Enter D'AMVILLE, BELFOREST, LEVIDULCIA, ROUSARD, CASTABELLA, LANGUEBEAU SNUFF *at one door; at the other door* CATAPLASMA *and* SOQUETTE, *ushered by* FRESCO.

134–5 See Textual note, p. 196.

140 *the proverb*: M.P. Tilley, *A Dictionary of Proverbs in England in the Sixteenth and Seventeenth Centuries* (Ann Arbor, 1950), c380.

142 *ability*: in the sexual sense.

154 *winked*: ignored it by shutting his eyes to it.

LEVIDULCIA. Mistress Cataplasma! I expected you an hour since.

CATAPLASMA. Certain ladies at my house, madam, detained me; otherwise I had attended your ladyship sooner.

LEVIDULCIA. We are beholding to you for your company. My lord, I pray you bid these gentlewomen welcome: th'are my invited friends.

D'AMVILLE. Gentlewomen, y'are welcome. Pray sit down.

LEVIDULCIA. Fresco! By my lord D'Amville's leave I prithee go into the buttery. Thou shalt find some o'my men there. If they bid thee not welcome they are very loggerheads.

FRESCO. If your loggerheads will not your hogsheads shall, madam, if I get into the buttery. *Exit* FRESCO.

D'AMVILLE. That fellow's disposition to mirth should be our present example. Let's be grave and meditate when our affairs require our seriousness. 'Tis out of season to be heavily disposed.

LEVIDULCIA. We should be all wound up into the key of mirth.

D'AMVILLE. The music there.

BELFOREST. Where's my lord Montferrers? Tell him here's a room attends him.

Enter MONTFERRERS.

MONTFERRERS. Heaven give your marriage that I am deprived of – joy.

D'AMVILLE. My lord Belforest! Castabella's health!

D'AMVILLE *drinks.*

Set ope the cellar doors and let this health
Go freely round the house. Another to
Your son, my lord: to noble Charlemont.
He is a soldier. Let the instruments
Of war congratulate his memory.

Drums and trumpets.

Enter a servant.

---

2 *since*: ago.
13 *loggerheads*: idiots, blockheads.
24 *attends*: waits for.
28–44 See Textual note, p. 196.

SERVANT. My lord, here's one i'th'habit of a soldier says he is newly returned from Ostend and has some business of import to speak.

D'AMVILLE. Ostend! Let him come in. My soul foretells
He brings the news will make our music full.
My brother's joy would do't, and here comes he
Will raise it.

Enter BORACHIO *disguised.*

MONTFERRERS. O my spirit, it does dissuade
My tongue to question him, as if it knew
His answer would displease.

D'AMVILLE. Soldier, what news?
We heard a rumour of a blow you gave
The enemy.

BORACHIO. 'Tis very true, my lord.

BELFOREST. Canst thou relate it?

BORACHIO. Yes.

D'AMVILLE. I prithee do.

BORACHIO. The enemy, defeated of a fair
Advantage by a flatt'ring stratagem,
Plants all th'artillery against the town;
Whose thunder and lightning made our bulwarks shake,
And threat'nèd in that terrible report
The storm wherewith they meant to second it.
The assault was general; but for the place
That promised most advantage to be forced
The pride of all their army was drawn forth
And equally divided into front
And rear. They marched. And, coming to a stand,
Ready to pass our channel at an ebb,
W'advised it for our safest course to draw
Our sluices up and make't unpassable.
Our governor opposed, and suffered 'em
To charge us home e'en to the rampier's foot.
But when their front was forcing up our breach
At push o'pike, then did his policy

---

34 *Ostend*: was besieged from 1601–1604.
35 *import*: importance.
55 *stand*: halt.
57–8 *draw . . . sluices*: open our floodgates.
60 *rampier*: here 'dam'.
62 *policy*: here 'tactic'.

Let go the sluices and tripped up the heels
Of the whole body of their troop that stood
Within the violent current of the stream.
Their front, beleaguered 'twixt the water and
The town, seeing the flood was grown too deep
To promise them a safe retreat, exposed
The force of all their spirits (like the last
Expiring gasp of a strong-hearted man)
Upon the hazard of one charge, but were
Oppressed and fell. The rest, that could not swim,
Were only drowned, but those that thought to 'scape
By swimming were, by murderers that flankered
The level of the flood, both drowned and slain.

D'AMVILLE. Now by my soul, soldier, a brave service.

MONTFERRERS. O what became of my dear Charlemont?

BORACHIO. Walking next day upon the fatal shore,
Among the slaughtered bodies of their men,
Which the full-stomached sea had cast upon
The sands, it was m'unhappy chance to light
Upon a face whose favour when it lived
My astonished mind informed me I had seen.
He lay in's armour, as if that had been
His coffin, and the weeping sea (like one
Whose milder temper doth lament the death
Of him whom in his rage he slew) runs up
The shore, embraces him, kisses his cheek,
Goes back again and forces up the sands
To bury him, and every time it parts
Sheds tears upon him, till at last (as if
It could no longer endure to see the man
Whom it had slain, yet loath to leave him) with
A kind of unresolved, unwilling pace,
Winding her waves one in another, like
A man that folds his arms or wrings his hands
For grief, ebbed from the body and descends,
As if it would sink down into the earth
And hide itself for shame of such a deed.

---

66 *beleaguered*: trapped.
71 *hazard*: chance.
74 *flankered*: flanked.
80 *full-stomached*: i.e. having devoured enough.
82 *favour*: appearance.

D'AMVILLE. And, soldier, who was this?
MONTFERRERS. O, Charlemont!
BORACHIO. Your fear hath told you that whereof my grief
Was loath to be the messenger.
CASTABELLA. O, God!

Exit CASTABELLA.

D'AMVILLE. Charlemont drowned? Why, how could that be, since it was the adverse party that received the overthrow?

BORACHIO. His forward spirit pressed into the front,
And, being engaged within the enemy,
When they retreated through the rising stream
I'the violent confusion of the throng
Was overborne and perished in the flood.
And here's the sad remembrance of his life

Shows the scarf.

Which for his sake I will for ever wear.
MONTFERRERS. Torment me not with witnesses of that
Which I desire not to believe, yet must.
D'AMVILLE. Thou art a screech-owl and dost come i'night
To be the cursèd messenger of death.
Away. Depart my house, or – by my soul –
You'll find me a more fatal enemy
Than ever was Ostend. Be gone. Dispatch.
BORACHIO. Sir, 'twas my love . . .
D'AMVILLE. Your love to vex my heart with that I hate?
Hark, do you hear, you knave?
(*Aside to Borachio*) O th'art a most delicate, sweet, eloquent villain.
BORACHIO. (*aside to D'Amville*) Was't not well counterfeited?
D'AMVILLE. (*aside to Borachio*) Rarely. (*Aloud*) Be gone, I will not hear reply.
BORACHIO. Why then farewell. I will not trouble you.

Exit BORACHIO.

D'AMVILLE. (*aside*) So. The foundation's laid. Now by degrees

---

104 *adverse*: opposing.
111 s.d. See Textual note, p. 196.
115 *screech-owl*: traditionally indicative of ill fortune.
125–6 *counterfeited*: acted, imitated.

The work will rise and soon be perfected.
(*Aloud*) O, this uncertain fate of mortal man!

BELFOREST. What then? It is the inevitable fate
Of all things underneath the moon.

D'AMVILLE. 'Tis true.
Brother, for health's sake overcome your grief.

MONTFERRERS. I cannot, sir, I am uncapable
Of comfort. My turn will be next. I feel
Myself not well.

D'AMVILLE. You yield too much to grief.

LANGUEBEAU. All men are mortal. The hour of death is uncertain. Age makes sickness the more dangerous. And grief is subject to distraction. You know not how soon you may deprived of the benefit of sense. In my understanding, therefore, you shall do well, if you be sick, to set your state in present order. Make your will.

D'AMVILLE. (*aside*) I have my wish. (*Aloud*) Lights for my brother.

MONTFERRERS. I'll withdraw a while
And crave the honest counsel of this man.

BELFOREST. With all my heart. I pray attend him, sir.

Exeunt MONTFERRERS *and* SNUFF.

This next room, please your lordship.

D'AMVILLE. Where you will.

Exeunt BELFOREST *and* D'AMVILLE.

LEVIDULCIA. My daughter's gone. Come son. Mistress Cataplasma, come, we'll up into her chamber. I'd fain see how she entertains the expectation of her husband's bedfellowship.

ROUSARD. 'Faith, howsoever she entertains it, I shall hardly please her; therefore let her rest.

LEVIDULCIA. Nay, please her hardly and you please her best.

Exeunt all.

SCENE II

Enter three servants drunk, drawing in FRESCO.

1 SERVANT. Boy! Fill some drink, boy.

FRESCO. Enough, good sir, not a drop more, by this light.

---

157 *hardly*: Levidulcia picks up Rousard's 'hardly' (scarcely) and converts its meaning into the sexual sense of 'passionately'.

2 SERVANT. Not by this light? Why then put out the candles and we'll drink in the dark and t'wou't, old boy.

FRESCO. No, no, no, no, no.

3 SERVANT. Why then take thy liquor. A health, Fresco. *Kneels.*

FRESCO. Your health will make me sick, sir.

1 SERVANT. Then 'twill bring you o'your knees I hope, sir

FRESCO. May I not stand and pledge it, sir?

2 SERVANT. I hope you will do as we do.

FRESCO. Nay, then indeed I must not stand, for you cannot.

3 SERVANT. Well said, old boy.

FRESCO. Old boy! You'll make me a young child anon, for if I continue this I shall scarce be able to go alone.

1 SERVANT. My body is as weak as water, Fresco.

FRESCO. Good reason, sir – the beer has sent all the malt up into your brain and left nothing but the water in your body.

Enter D'AMVILLE *and* BORACHIO *closely observing their drunkenness.*

D'AMVILLE. Borachio, see'st those fellows?

BORACHIO. Yes, my lord.

D'AMVILLE. Their drunkenness, that seems ridiculous,
Shall be a serious instrument to bring
Our sober purposes to their success.

BORACHIO. I am prepared for the execution, sir.

D'AMVILLE. Cast off this habit, and about it straight.

BORACHIO. Let them drink healths and drown their brains i'the flood;
I'll promise them they shall be pledged in blood.

Exit BORACHIO.

1 SERVANT. You ha'left a damnable snuff here.

2 SERVANT. Do you take that in snuff, sir?

1 SERVANT. You are a damnable rogue then.

Together by the ears.

---

4 *t'wou't*: see Textual note, p. 196.
10 *pledge*: toast.
16 *go*: walk.
26 *habit*: costume.
29 *snuff*: the dregs or lees at the bottom of a cup.
30 Are you offended by that? (proverbial).

D'AMVILLE. (*aside*) Fortune I honour thee. My plot still rises
According to the model of mine own desires.
(*Aloud*) Lights for my brother. What, ha'you drunk yourselves mad, you knaves?

1 SERVANT. My lord, the jacks abused me.

D'AMVILLE. I think they are the jacks indeed that have abused thee. Dost hear? That fellow is a proud knave; he has abused thee. As thou goest over the fields by and by, in lighting my brother home, I'll tell thee what sha't do. Knock him over the pate with thy torch: I'll bear thee out in't.

1 SERVANT. I will singe the goose, by this torch.

Exit 1 servant.

D'AMVILLE. (*to 2 servant*) Dost hear, fellow? See'st thou that proud knave? I have given him a lesson for his sauciness. H'as wronged thee. I'll tell thee what shalt do: as we go over the fields by and by clap him suddenly over the coxcomb with thy torch: I'll bear thee out in't.

2 SERVANT. I will make him understand as much.

Exit 2 servant.

Enter LANGUEBEAU SNUFF.

D'AMVILLE. Now, monsieur Snuff, what has my brother done?

LANGUEBEAU. Made his will, and by that will made you his heir, with this proviso, that as occasion shall hereafter move him he may revoke or alter it when he pleases.

D'AMVILLE. (*aside*) Yes, let him if he can. I'll make it sure from his revoking.

Enter MONTFERRERS *and* BELFOREST, *attended with lights.*

MONTFERRERS. Brother, now good night.

36–8 (a) jacks = knaves (the terms are still interchangeable for the third court card in card games); (b) D'Amville at l. 34 plays on the double sense of jacks = knaves, and jacks = large drinking vessels.

41 *pate*: head.

48 *coxcomb*: head.

54 *proviso*: condition, provision.

D'AMVILLE. The sky is dark, we'll bring you o'er the fields.
(*Aside*) Who can but strike wants wisdom to maintain:
He that strikes safe and sure has heart and brain.
Exeunt all.

SCENE III

Enter CASTABELLA *alone.*

CASTABELLA. O love, thou chaste affection of the soul,
Without th'adult'rate mixture of the blood;
That virtue which to goodness addeth good;
The minion of heaven's heart. Heaven, is't my fate
For loving that thou lov'st to get thy hate?
Or was my Charlemont thy chosen love,
And therefore hast received him to thyself?
Then I confess thy anger's not unjust:
I was thy rival. Yet to be divorced
From love has been a punishment enough,
Sweet heaven, without being married unto hate,
Hadst thou been pleased. O double misery!
Yet since thy pleasure hath inflicted it,
If not my heart, my duty shall submit.

Enter LEVIDULCIA, ROUSARD, CATAPLASMA, SOQUETTE, *and* FRESCO *with a lantern.*

LEVIDULCIA. Mistress Cataplasma, good night. I pray when your man has brought you home let him return and light me to my house.

CATAPLASMA. He shall instantly wait on your ladyship.

LEVIDULCIA. Good, mistress Cataplasma, for my servants are all drunk – I cannot be beholding to 'em for their attendance.

Exeunt CATAPLASMA, SOQUETTE *and* FRESCO.

O here's your bride.

ROUSARD. And melancholic too
Methinks.

LEVIDULCIA. How can she choose? Your sickness will
Distaste th'expected sweetness o'the night:

---

2 *adult'rate*: debasing.
4 *minion*: beloved.
9–12 See Textual note, p. 196.
20 *beholding to*: dependent on.

That makes her heavy.
ROUSARD. That should make her light.
LEVIDULCIA. Look you to that.
CASTABELLA. What sweetness speak you of?
The sweetness of the night consists in rest.
ROUSARD. With that sweetness thou shalt be surely blessed
Unless my groaning wake thee. Do not moan.
LEVIDULCIA. Sh'ad rather you would wake and make her groan.
ROUSARD. Nay, troth, sweetheart, I will not trouble thee:
Thou shalt not lose thy maidenhead tonight.
CASTABELLA. O might that weakness ever be in force
I never would desire to sue divorce!
ROUSARD. Wilt go to bed?
CASTABELLA. I will attend you, sir.
ROUSARD. Mother, good night.
LEVIDULCIA. Pleasure be your bedfellow.

Exeunt ROUSARD *and* CASTABELLA.

Why sure their generation was asleep
When she begot those dormice, that she made
Them up so weakly and imperfectly.
One wants desire; the tother ability.
When my affection even with their cold bloods
(As snow rubbed through an active hand does make
The flesh to burn) by agitation is
Inflamed. I could unbrace and entertain
The air to cool it.

Enter SEBASTIAN.

SEBASTIAN. That but mitigates
The heat: rather embrace and entertain
A younger brother: he can quench the fire.
LEVIDULCIA. Can you so, sir? Now I beshrew your ear.

---

25 *heavy*: sad.
light: Rousard means that because of his sickness Castabella will not have to bear his body's weight. Levidulcia (l. 26) means that this weight should make Castabella wanton.
30 *groan*: in sexual passion.
37 *generation*: procreative force (here personified as 'she').
41 *affection*: passion.
44 *unbrace*: undress.
48 *beshrew*: scold.

Why, bold Sebastian, how dare you approach
So near the presence of your displeased father?

SEBASTIAN. Under the protection of his present absence.

LEVIDULCIA. Belike you knew he was abroad then.

SEBASTIAN. Yes.
Let me encounter you so: I'll persuade
Yours means to reconcile me to his love.

LEVIDULCIA. Is that the way? I understand you not.
But for your reconcilement meet m'at home:
I'll satisfy your suit.

SEBASTIAN. Within this half hour?

LEVIDULCIA. Or within this whole hour. When you will.

Exit SEBASTIAN.

A lusty blood! Has both the presence and the spirit of a man. I like the freedom of his behaviour. Ho, Sebastian! Gone? Has set my blood a-boiling i'my veins, and now, like water poured upon the ground, that mixes itself with every moisture it meets, I could clasp with any man.

Enter FRESCO *with a lantern.*

O Fresco, art thou come? (*Aside*) If tother fail, then thou art entertained.
Lust is a spirit, which whosoe'er doth raise,
The next man that encounters boldly lays.

Exeunt LEVIDULCIA *and* FRESCO.

SCENE IV

Enter BORACHIO *warily and hastily over the stage, with a stone in either hand.*

BORACHIO. Such stones men use to raise a house upon,
But with these stones I go to ruin one. *Descends.*

Enter two servants drunk, fighting with their torches; D'AMVILLE, MONTFERRERS, BELFOREST *and* LANGUEBEAU SNUFF.

BELFOREST. Passion o'me, you drunken knaves, you'll put the lights out.

D'AMVILLE. No, my lord, th'are but in jest.

---

69 *lays*: i.e. lays the spirit to rest by 'laying' the woman sexually.

1 SERVANT. Mine's out.

D'AMVILLE. Then light it at his head, that's light enough. 'Fore God th'are out. You drunken rascals, back and light 'em.

Exeunt servants.

BELFOREST. 'Tis exceeding dark.

D'AMVILLE. No matter. I am acquainted with the way. Your hand. Let's easily walk. I'll lead you till they come.

MONTFERRERS. My soul's oppressed with grief. 'T lies heavy at my heart. O my departed son, ere long I shall be with thee.

D'Amville thrusts him down into the gravel pit.

D'AMVILLE. Marry, God forbid!

MONTFERRERS. O, O, O.

D'AMVILLE. Now all the host of heaven forbid! Knaves, rogues!

BELFOREST. Pray God he be not hurt: he's fallen into the gravel pit.

D'AMVILLE. Brother, dear brother! Rascals, villains, knaves!

Enter the servants with lights.

Eternal darkness damn you. Come away.
Go round about into the gravel pit
And help my brother up. Why, what a strange
Unlucky night is this! Is't not, my lord?
I think that dog that howled the news of grief,
That fatal screech-owl, ushered on this mischief.

Enter the servants with the murdered body.

LANGUEBEAU. Mischief indeed, my lord, your brother's dead.

BELFOREST. He's dead.

SERVANT. He's dead.

D'AMVILLE. Dead be your tongues! Drop out
Mine eye-balls and let envious fortune play

7–23 See Textual note, p. 197.

29 *screech-owl*: see above II.i.115 n.

31–3 *Drop . . . with'em*: something of a Renaissance commonplace (see e.g. Webster's *Duchess of Malfi* V.iv.53–4, ed. Brennan).

31ff. See Textual note, p. 197.

At tennis with'em. Have I lived to this?
Malicious nature, hadst thou borne me blind
Th'adst yet been something favourable to me.
No breath? No motion? 'Prithee tell me, heaven,
Hast shut thine eye to wink at murder, or
Hast put this sable garment on to mourn
At's death? Not one poor spark in the whole spacious
sky,
Of all that endless number, would vouchsafe
To shine? You viceroys to the king of nature,
Whose constellations govern mortal births,
Where is that fatal planet ruled at his
Nativity? That might ha'pleased to light
Him out as well into the world, unless
It be ashamed t'have been th'instrument
Of such a good man's cursèd destiny.

BELFOREST. Passion transports you. Recollect yourself.
Lament him not. Whether our deaths be good
Or bad it is not death but life that tries:
He lived well, therefore, questionless, well dies.

D'AMVILLE. Ay, 'tis an easy thing for him that has no pain
To talk of patience. Do you think that nature
Has no feeling?

BELFOREST. Feeling? Yes. But has she
Purposed anything for nothing? What good
Receives this body by your grief? Whether
Is't more unnatural not to grieve for him
You cannot help with it, or hurt yourself
With grieving and yet grieve in vain?

D'AMVILLE. Indeed,
Had he been taken from me like a piece
O'dead flesh I should neither ha'felt it
Nor grieved for't. But come hither, pray look here.
Behold the lively tincture of his blood!
Neither the dropsy or the jaundice in't,
But the true freshness of a sanguine red,

---

37 *wink*: connive.
39 *spark*: i.e. of starlight.
50 *tries*: decides the issue.
65 *sanguine*: here 'healthy' (in Elizabethan physiology a sanguine complexion was a sign of a lively temperament).

For all the fog of this black murd'rous night
Has mixed with it. For anything I know
He might ha'lived till doomsday and ha'done
More good than either you or I. O brother!
He was a man of such a native goodness
As if regeneration had been given
Him in his mother's womb; so harmless that
Rather than ha'trod upon a worm he
Would ha'shunned the way; so dearly pitiful
That ere the poor could ask his charity
With dry eyes, he gave 'em relief wi'tears,
With tears, yes, faith, with tears.

BELFOREST. Take up the corpse.
For wisdom's sake let reason fortify
This weakness.

D'AMVILLE. Why, what would you ha'me do?
Foolish nature will have her course in spite
O'wisdom. But I have e'en done. All these
Words were but a great wind and now this shower
Of tears has laid it I am calm again.
You may set forward when you will. I'll follow
Like one that must and would not.

LANGUEBEAU. Our opposition will but trouble him.

BELFOREST. The grief that melts to tears by itself is spent,
Passion resisted grows more violent.

Exeunt all. D'AMVILLE *remains;* BORACHIO *ascends.*

D'AMVILLE. Here's a sweet comedy. 'T begins with
'O dolentis' and concludes with ha, ha, he!

BORACHIO. Ha, ha, he!

D'AMVILLE. O my echo, I could stand
Reverberating this sweet musical
Air of joy till I had perished my sound
Lungs with violent laughter.
Lovely night-raven, th'ast seized a carcass.

BORACHIO. Put him out on's pain. I lay so fitly

---

66 *for all*: although.
74 *shunned*: avoided.
88 s.d. The gravel pit from which Borachio now returns to the stage was probably represented by the yard beside the platform.
90 *'O dolentis'*: 'The O of one in pain'.
92 *Reverberating*: echoing.

Underneath the bank from whence he fell that
Ere his falt'ring tongue could utter double
'O' I knocked out's brains with this fair ruby,
And had another stone just of this form
And bigness ready that I laid i'the
Broken skull upo'the ground for's pillow,
Against the which they thought he fell and perished.

D'AMVILLE. Upon this ground I'll build my manor house
And this shall be the chiefest corner-stone.

BORACHIO. 'T has crowned the most judicious murder that
The brain of man was e'er delivered of.

D'AMVILLE. Ay, mark the plot. Not any circumstance
That stood within the reach of the design
Of persons, dispositions, matter, time,
Or place, but by this brain of mine was made
An instrumental help, yet nothing from
Th'induction to th'accomplishment seemed force
Or done on purpose, but by accident.

BORACHIO. First my report that Charlemont was dead,
Though false yet covered with a mask of truth.

D'AMVILLE. Ay, and delivered in as fit a time,
When all our minds so wholly were possessed
With one affair that no man would suspect
A thought employed for any second end.

BORACHIO. Then the precisian to be ready, when
Your brother spake of death, to move his will.

D'AMVILLE. His business called him thither, and it fell
Within his office, unrequested to it.
From him it came religiously and saved
Our project from suspicion, which if I
Had moved had been endangered.

BORACHIO. Then your healths;

---

99 *ruby*: here 'blood-stained rock'.
108 *mark*: pay attention to.
109 *reach of the design*: scope of this plot.
110 *dispositions*: arrangements.
113 *induction*: inception.
121 *precisian*: i.e. Languebeau (Puritans were often called precisians because of their concern for the details of biblical texts). Priests often drafted wills for parishioners.
122 *move*: suggest he make.
124 *office*: function.

Though seeming but the ordinary rites
And ceremonies due to festivals . . .
D'AMVILLE. Yet used by me to make the servants drunk.
An instrument the plot could not have missed.
'Twas easy to set drunkards by the ears:
Th'had nothing but torches to fight with,
And when those lights were out . . .
BORACHIO. Then darkness did
Protect the execution of the work
Both from prevention and discovery.
D'AMVILLE. Here was a murder bravely carried through
The eye of observation, unobserved.
BORACHIO. And those that saw the passage of it made
The instruments, yet knew not what they did.
D'AMVILLE. That power of rule philosophers ascribe
To him they call the supreme of the stars,
Making their influences governors
Of sublunary creatures, when their selves
Are senseless of their operations.
Thunder and lightning.
What, dost start at thunder? Credit my belief,
'Tis a mere effect of nature; an exhalation
Hot and dry involved within a wat'ry vapour
I'the middle region of the air, whose
Coldness congealing that thick moisture to
A cloud, the angry exhalation shut
Within a prison of contrary quality
Strives to be free, and with the violent
Eruption through the grossness of that
Cloud makes this noise we hear.
BORACHIO. 'Tis a fearful noise.
D'AMVILLE. 'Tis a brave noise, and methinks graces
Our accomplished project as a peal of
Ord'nance does a triumph. It speaks encouragement.
Now nature shows thee how it favoured our

---

131 *missed*: have done without.
137–8 *bravely . . . observation*: explained by the word 'unobserved'.
141ff. See Textual note, p. 197.
142 i.e. God.
144 *sublunary*: mundane (literally 'beneath the stars').
145 *senseless*: unaware.
146ff. See Additional note, p. 198.
159 *Ord'nance*: artillery.

Performance, to forbear this noise when we
Set forth because it should not terrify
My brother's going home, which would have dashed
Our purpose; to forbear this lightning in
Our passage lest it should ha'warned him o'
The pitfall. Then propitious nature
Winked at our proceedings: now it doth express
How that forbearance favoured our success.

BORACHIO. You have confirmed me. For it follows well
That nature (since herself decay doth hate)
Should favour those that strengthen their estate.

D'AMVILLE. Our next endeavour is – since on the false
Report that Charlemont is dead depends
The fabric of the work – to credit that
With all the countenance we can.

BORACHIO. Faith, sir,
Even let his own inheritance, whereof
Y'ave dispossessed him, countenance the act.
Spare so much out of that to give him a
Solemnity of funeral. 'Twill quit
The cost and make your apprehension of
His death appear more confident and true.

D'AMVILLE. I'll take thy counsel. Now farewell black night,
Thou beauteous mistress of a murderer:
To honour thee that hast accomplished all
I'll wear thy colours at his funeral.

Exeunt D'AMVILLE *and* BORACHIO.

SCENE V

Enter LEVIDULCIA *into her chamber, manned by* FRESCO.

LEVIDULCIA. Y'are welcome into my chamber, Fresco. Prithee shut the door. Nay, thou mistakest me – come in and shut it.

---

161 *forbear*: abstain from.
169 *confirmed*: convinced.
174–5 *credit . . . can*: make this false report seem as convincing as possible.
179 *quit*: cover.
181 *confident*: convincing.

FRESCO. 'Tis somewhat late, madam.
LEVIDULCIA. No matter. I have something to say to thee. What, is not thy mistress towards a husband yet?
FRESCO. Faith, madam, she has suitors But they will not suit her methinks: they will not come off lustily it seems.
LEVIDULCIA. They will not come on lustily, thou wouldst say.
FRESCO. I mean, madam, they are not rich enough.
LEVIDULCIA. But I, Fresco, they are not bold enough. Thy mistress is of a lively, attractive blood, Fresco, and, in troth, she's o'my mind for that. A poor spirit is poorer than a poor purse. Give me a fellow that brings not only temptation with him, but has the activity of wit and audacity of spirit to apply every word and gesture of a woman's speech and behaviour to his own desire, and make her believe she's the suitor herself, never give back till he has made her yield to it.
FRESCO. Indeed, among our equals, madam, but otherwise we shall be horribly put out o'countenance.
LEVIDULCIA. Thou art deceived, Fresco. Ladies are as courteous as yeomen's wives and, methinks, they should be more gentle. Hot diet and soft ease makes 'em, like wax always kept warm, more easy to take impression. Prithee untie my shoe. What, art thou shamefaced too? Go roundly to work man, my leg is not gouty – 'twill endure the feeling, I warrant thee. Come hither, Fresco, thine ear. 'Sdainty, I mistook thine ear and hit thy lip.
FRESCO. Your ladyship has made me blush.
LEVIDULCIA. That shows th'art full o'lusty blood and thou knowest not how to use it. Let me see thy hand. Thou shouldst not be shamefaced by thy hand, Fresco. Here's a brawny flesh and a hairy skin: both signs of

---

8–11 Fresco explains his 'come off lustily' in his next line, while Levidulcia suggests that he means that the suitors fail to show enough sexual boldness.
13 *I*: see Textual note, p. 197.
24 *out o'countenance*: humiliated.
30 *roundly*: confidently.
32 *'Sdainty*: By God's dignity.

an able body. I do not like these phlegmatic, smooth-skinned, soft-fleshed fellows. They are like candied suckets when they begin to perish, which I would always empty my closet of and give 'em my chamber-maid. I have some skill in palmistry: by this line that stands directly against me thou shouldst be near a good fortune, Fresco, if thou hadst the grace to entertain it.

FRESCO. O what is that, madam, I pray?

LEVIDULCIA. No less than the love of a fair lady, if thou dost not lose her with faint-heartedness.

FRESCO. A lady, madam? Alas, a lady is a great thing: I cannot compass her.

LEVIDULCIA. No? Why? I am a lady. Am I so great I cannot be compassed? Clasp my waist and try.

FRESCO. I could find i'my heart, madam . . .

SEBASTIAN *knocks within.*

LEVIDULCIA. 'Ud's body, my husband! Faint-hearted fool! I think thou wert begotten between the North Pole and the congealed passage. Now, like an ambitious coward that betrays himself with fearful delay, you must suffer for the treason you never committed. Go, hide thyself behind yond'arras, instantly.

FRESCO *hides himself.*

Enter SEBASTIAN.

Sebastian! What do you here so late?

SEBASTIAN. Nothing yet, but I hope I shall. *Kisses her.*

LEVIDULCIA. Y'are very bold.

SEBASTIAN. And you very valiant, for you meet me at full career.

LEVIDULCIA. You come to ha'me move thy father's reconciliation? I'll write a word or two i'your behalf.

---

39 *phlegmatic*: phlegm, one of the four humours, was associated with sluggishness and self-restraint.

41 *suckets*: fruit preserved in sugar.

53 *compassed*: (a) embraced, (b) obtained.

55 *'Ud's body*: God's body.

57 *congealed passage*: probably, as Ribner suggests, a reference to Hudson's discovery in 1607 of the N.E. passage to China.

60 *arras*: tapestry.

65 *full career*: a tilting term meaning 'at full speed'.

SEBASTIAN. A word or two, madam? That you do for me will not be contained in less than the compass of two sheets. But, in plain terms, shall we take the opportunity of privateness?

LEVIDULCIA. What to do?

SEBASTIAN. To dance the beginning of the world after the English manner.

LEVIDULCIA. Why not after the French or Italian?

SEBASTIAN. Fie, they dance it preposterously – backward.

LEVIDULCIA. Are you so active to dance?

SEBASTIAN. I can shake my heels.

LEVIDULCIA. Y'are well made for't.

SEBASTIAN. Measure me from top to toe, you shall not find me differ much from the true standard of proportion.

BELFOREST *knocks within.*

LEVIDULCIA. I think I am accursed, Sebastian! There's one at the door has beaten opportunity away from us. In brief, I love thee. And it shall not be long before I give thee a testimony of it. To save thee now from suspicion do no more but draw thy rapier, chafe thyself, and when he comes in rush by without taking notice of him. Only seem to be angry and let me alone for the rest.

Enter BELFOREST.

SEBASTIAN. Now by the hand of Mercury!

Exit SEBASTIAN.

BELFOREST. What's the matter, wife?

LEVIDULCIA. O, O, husband!

BELFOREST. Prithee, what ail'st thou, woman?

LEVIDULCIA. O feel my pulse. It beats I warrant you. Be patient a little, sweet husband; tarry but till my breath come to me again and I'll satisfy you.

69–70 Sebastian is, of course, punning on sheets of paper/bedsheets.

73–6 Sebastian's first line simply means 'to have ordinary sexual intercourse': Levidulcia's comment and Sebastian's reply to it refer to the common association of anal intercourse with the French and Italians.

76 *preposterously*: with a pun – (a) outrageously; (b) backside forward.

87–8 *chafe thyself*: make yourself seem angry.

96 *tarry*: wait.

BELFOREST. What ails Sebastian? He looks so distractedly.

LEVIDULCIA. The poor gentleman's almost out on's wits I think. You remember the displeasure his father took against him about the liberty of speech he used even now when your daughter went to be married?

BELFOREST. Yes, what of that?

LEVIDULCIA. 'Thas crazed him sure. He met a poor man in the street even now. Upon what quarrel I know not, but he pursued him so violently that if my house had not been his rescue he had surely killed him.

BELFOREST. What a strange, desperate young man is that!

LEVIDULCIA. Nay husband, he grew so in rage when he saw the man was conveyed from him that he was ready even to have drawn his naked weapon upon me. And had not your knocking at the door prevented him surely h'ad done something to me.

BELFOREST. Where's the man?

LEVIDULCIA. Alas, here. I warrant you the poor fearful fool is scarce come to himself again yet. (*Aside*) If the fool have any wit he will apprehend me. (*To Fresco*) Do you hear, sir? You may be bold to come forth: the fury that haunted you is gone.

FRESCO *peeps fearfully forth from behind the arras, then enters.*

FRESCO. Are you sure he is gone?

BELFOREST. He's gone, he's gone, I warrant thee.

FRESCO. I would I were gone too. H'as shook me almost into a dead palsy.

BELFOREST. How fell the difference between you?

FRESCO. I would I were out at the back door.

BELFOREST. Th'art safe enough. Prithee tell's the falling out.

FRESCO. Yes, sir, when I have recovered my spirits. My memory is almost frighted from me. O, so, so, so. Why, sir, as I came along the street, sir, this same gentleman came stumbling after me and trod o'my heel. I cried 'O'. 'Do you cry, sirrah?', says he. 'Let me see your heel; if it be not hurt I'll make you cry for something.' So he claps my head between his legs and pulls off my

111 *naked weapon*: double meaning – (a) sword; (b) penis.
117 *apprehend*: understand.

shoe. I having shifted no socks in a sennight the gentleman cried 'Foh', and said my feet were base and cowardly feet, they stunk for fear. Then he knocked my shoe about my pate and I cried 'O' once more. In the meantime comes a shag-haired dog by and rubs against his shins. The gentleman took the dog in shag-hair to be some watchman in a rug-gown and swore he would hang me up at the next door with my lantern in my hand that passengers might see their way as they went, without rubbing against gentlemen's shins. So, for want of a cord, he took his own garters off and as he was going to make a noose I watched my time and ran away. And as I ran, indeed, I bid him hang himself in his own garters. So he, in choler, pursued me hither, as you can see.

BELFOREST. Why, this savours of distraction.

LEVIDULCIA. Of mere distraction.

FRESCO. (*aside*) Howsoever it savours I am sure it smells like a lie.

BELFOREST. Thou mayst go forth at the back door, honest fellow, the way is private and safe.

FRESCO. So it had need, for your fore-door is both common and dangerous.

Exit BELFOREST.

LEVIDULCIA. Goodnight, honest Fresco.

FRESCO. Goodnight, madam. (*Aside*) If you get me kissing o'ladies again . . . *Exit* FRESCO.

LEVIDULCIA. This falls out handsomely.
But yet the matter does not well succeed
Till I have brought it to the very deed.

Exit LEVIDULCIA.

SCENE VI

Enter CHARLEMONT *in arms, a soldier and a sergeant.*

---

135 *shifted*: changed.
sennight: week (seven-night).
139 *shag-haired*: rough-haired.
141 *rug-gown*: a coarse coat of rough wool.
151 *mere*: complete, total.
156 *fore-door*: double meaning – (a) front door; (b) wife's vagina.
II.vi. s.d. See Textual note, p. 197.

CHARLEMONT. Sergeant, what hour o'the night is't?
SERGEANT. About one.
CHARLEMONT. I would you would relieve me, for I am
So heavy that I shall ha'much ado
To stand out my perdu.

Thunder and lightning.

SERGEANT. I'll e'en but walk
The round, sir, and then presently return.

SOLDIER. For God's sake, sergeant, relieve me: above five hours together in so foul a stormy night as this?

SERGEANT. Why, 'tis a music, soldier. Heaven and earth are now in consort when the thunder and the cannon play to one another. *Exit sergeant.*

CHARLEMONT. I know not why I should be thus inclined to sleep. I feel my disposition pressed with a necessity of heaviness. Soldier, if thou hast any better eyes, I prithee wake me when the sergeant comes.

SOLDIER. Sir, 'tis so dark and stormy that I shall scarce either see or hear him ere he comes upon me.

CHARLEMONT. I cannot force myself to wake.

Sleeps.

Enter the ghost of MONTFERRERS.

MONTFERRERS. Return to France, for thy old father's dead,
And thou by murder disinheritèd.
Attend with patience the success of things
But leave revenge unto the king of kings. *Exit ghost.*

CHARLEMONT *starts and wakes.*

CHARLEMONT. O my affrighted soul, what fearful dream
Was this that waked me? Dreams are but the raised
Impressions of premeditated things,
By serious apprehension left upon
Our minds, or else th'imaginary shapes

---

5 *perdu*: difficult outpost duty.
6 *round*: i.e. of the outposts.
presently: at once.
10 *in consort*: (a) in harmony; (b) in musical unity.
22 The key biblical text for this line is *Romans* 12;19 ('Vengeance is mine, I will repay, saith the Lord').
24ff. Collins (*The Plays and Poems of Cyril Tourneur*, 1875) refers this explanation of dreams to Lodge's *A Fig for Momus* and Chapman's *Revenge of Bussy* V.i.

Of objects proper to the complexion, or
The dispositions of our bodies. These
Can neither of them be the cause why I
Should dream thus, for my mind has not been moved
With any one conception of a thought
To such a purpose, nor my nature wont
To trouble me with fantasies of terror.
It must be something that my genius would
Inform me of. Now gracious heaven forbid!
O let my spirit be deprived of all
Foresight and knowledge ere it understand
That vision acted, or divine that act
To come. Why should I think so? Left I not
My worthy father i'the kind regard
Of a most loving uncle? – Soldier, saw'st
No apparition of a man?

SOLDIER. You dream, sir, I saw nothing.

CHARLEMONT. Tush. These idle dreams
Are fabulous. Our boiling fantasies
Like troubled waters falsify the shapes
Of things retained in them, and make 'em seem
Confounded when they are distinguished. So
My actions, daily conversant with war,
The argument of blood and death, had left,
Perhaps, th'imaginary presence of
Some bloody accident upon my mind,
Which, mixed confusedly with other thoughts,
Whereof th'remembrance of my father might
Be one, presented all together, seem
Incorporate, as if his body were
The owner of that blood, the subject of
That death, when he's at Paris and that blood
Shed here. It may be thus. I would not leave
The war, for reputation's sake, upon
An idle apprehension, a vain dream.

---

28 *complexion*: the combination of the humours in a body.
33 *wont*: accustomed.
35 *genius*: controlling spirit.
46 *fabulous*: imaginary.
49 *Confounded*: mixed, mingled.
50 *conversant*: accustomed.
57 *Incorporate*: united, of one piece.

Enter the ghost of MONTFERRERS.

SOLDIER. Stand, stand, I say. No? Why then have at thee. Sir, if you will not stand I'll make you fall. Nor stand nor fall? Nay then the devil's dam has broke her husband's head, for sure it is a spirit: I shot it through and yet it will not fall.

Exit soldier. The ghost approaches CHARLEMONT. *He fearfully avoids it.*

CHARLEMONT. O pardon me, my doubtful heart was slow
To credit that which I did fear to know.

Exit CHARLEMONT.

ACT III

SCENE I

Enter the funeral of Montferrers, D'AMVILLE.

D'AMVILLE. Set down the body. Pay earth what she lent:
But she shall bear a lasting monument,
To let succeeding ages truly know
That she is satisfied what he did owe,
Both principal and use, because his worth
Was better at his death than at his birth.

A dead march. Enter the funeral of Charlemont as a soldier.

And with his body place that memory
Of noble Charlemont, his worthy son.
And give their graves the rites that do belong
To soldiers. They were soldiers both. The father
Held open war with sin; the son with blood:
This in a war more gallant, that more good.

The first volley.

There place their arms and here their epitaphs,
And may these lines survive the last of graves.

---

68 *doubtful*: doubting.
69 *credit*: believe.
5 *use*: interest.
14 For this commonplace idea cf. Shakespeare *Sonnet* 55.

Reads the epitaph of Montferrers.

Here lie the ashes of that earth and fire
Whose heat and fruit did feed and warm the poor:
And they (as if they would in sighs expire
And into tears dissolve) his death deplore.
He did that good freely, for goodness' sake,
Unforced; for gen'rousness he held so dear
That he feared none but him that did him make
And yet he served him more for love than fear:
  So's life provided that, though he did die
  A sudden death, yet died not suddenly.

Reads the epitaph of Charlemont.

His body lies interred within this mould,
Who died a young man, yet departed old,
And all in strength of youth that man can have
Was ready still to drop into his grave.
For aged in virtue with a youthful eye
He welcomed it, being still prepared to die;
And living so, though young deprived of breath,
He did not suffer an untimely death.
But we may say of his brave, blessed decease:
He died in war and yet he died in peace.

The second volley.

O might that fire revive the ashes of
This phoenix! Yet the wonder would not be
So great as he was good, and wond'red at
For that. His life's example was so true
A practique of religion's theory
That her divinity seemed rather the
Description than th'instruction of his life.
And of his goodness was his virtuous son
A worthy imitator: so that on
These two Herculean pillars, where their arms

---

15 *Here lie*: a traditional epitaph formula (*hic jacet*).

23–32 For the idea of these lines see Jonson's 'To the immortal memory . . . of . . . Sir Lucius Cary' ll. 21ff.

30 *still*: at any time.

36 *phoenix*: the phoenix was fabled to burn itself to death, being reborn from its own ashes and thus immortal.

39 *practique*: practical illustration.

44 Hercules set up two pillars at the Gibraltar straits to prevent the seas beyond them being explored.

Are placed, there may be writ *Non ultra*. For
Beyond their lives, as well for youth as age,
Nor young nor old, in merit or in name,
Shall e'er exceed their virtues or their fame.

The third volley.

(*Aside*) 'Tis done. Thus fair accompliments make foul
Deeds gracious. Charlemont, come now when t'wout,
I've buried under these two marble stones
Thy living hopes and thy dead father's bones.

Exit D'AMVILLE.

Enter CASTABELLA, *mourning, to the monument of Charlemont.*

CASTABELLA. O thou that know'st me justly Charlemont's,
Though in the forced possession of another,
Since from thine own free spirit we receive it
That our affections cannot be compelled,
Though our actions may, be not displeased if on
The altar of his tomb I sacrifice
My tears. They are the jewels of my love
Dissolved into grief, and fall upon
His blasted spring as April dew upon
A sweet young blossom shaked before the time.

Enter CHARLEMONT *with a servant.*

CHARLEMONT. Go, see my trunks disposed of: I'll but walk
A turn or two i'the church and follow you.

Exit servant.

O here's the fatal monument of my
Dead father first presented to mine eye.
What's here? In memory of Charlemont?
Some false relation has abused belief.
I am deluded. (*Seeing Castabella*) But I thank thee, Heaven,
Forever let me be deluded thus.
My Castabella mourning o'er my hearse?
Sweet Castabella, rise, I am not dead.

---

45 *Non ultra*: no further.
49 *accompliments*: compliments.
50 *t'wout*: see II.ii.4 and Textual note, p. 197.
68 *relation*: account.

CASTABELLA. O heaven defend me! *Falls in a swoon.*
CHARLEMONT. I beshrew my rash
And inconsid'rate passion – Castabella!
That could not think – my Castabella! – that
My sudden presence might affright her sense.
I prithee, my affection, pardon me. *She rises.*
Reduce my understanding to thine eye.
Within this habit, which thy misinformed
Conceit takes only for a shape, live both
The soul and body of thy Charlemont.
CASTABELLA. I feel a substance, warm and soft and moist,
Subject to the capacity of sense.
CHARLEMONT. Which spirits are not, for their essence is
Above the nature and the order of
Those elements whereof our senses are
Created. Touch my lip. Why turn'st thou from me?
CASTABELLA. Grief above griefs! That which should woe relieve,
Wished and obtained, gives greater cause to grieve.
CHARLEMONT. Can Castabella think it cause of grief
That the relation of my death proves false?
CASTABELLA. The presence of the person we affect,
Being hopeless to enjoy him, makes our grief
More passionate than if we saw him not.
CHARLEMONT. Why not enjoy? Has absence changed thee?
CASTABELLA. Yes.
From maid to wife.
CHARLEMONT. Art married?
CASTABELLA. O, I am.
CHARLEMONT. Married? Had not my mother been a woman
I should protest against the chastity
Of all thy sex. How can the merchant or
The mariner, absent whole years from wives
Experienced in the satisfaction of
Desire, promise themselves to find their sheets
Unspotted with adultery at their

---

73 *beshrew*: blame.
80 *Conceit*: Imagination.
shape: ghost.
83 'able to receive sense-impressions'.

Return, when you that never had the sense
Of actual temptation could not stay
A few short months?

CASTABELLA. O, do but hear me speak.

CHARLEMONT. But thou wert wise, and didst consider that
A soldier might be maimed, and so – perhaps –
Lose his ability to please thee.

CASTABELLA. No.
That weakness pleases me in him I have.

CHARLEMONT. What? Married to a man unable too?
O strange incontinence! Why? Was thy blood
Increased to such a pleurisy of lust
That of necessity there must a vein
Be opened, though by one that had no skill
To do't?

CASTABELLA. Sir, I beseech you, hear me.

CHARLEMONT. Speak.

CASTABELLA. Heaven knows I am unguilty of this act.

CHARLEMONT. Why? Wert thou forced to do it?

CASTABELLA. Heaven knows I was.

CHARLEMONT. What villain did it?

CASTABELLA. Your uncle D'Amville.
And he that dispossessed my love of you
Hath disinherited you of possession.

CHARLEMONT. Disinherited? Wherein have I deserved
To be deprived of my dear father's love?

CASTABELLA. Both of his love and him. His soul's at rest,
But here your injured patience may behold
The signs of his lamented memory.

CHARLEMONT *finds his father's monument.*

'Has found it. When I took him for a ghost
I could endure the torment of my fear
More eas'ly than I can his sorrows bear.

Exit CASTABELLA.

CHARLEMONT. Of all men's griefs must mine be singular,
Without example? Here I met my grave –
And all men's woes are buried i'their graves

---

111 *unable*: impotent.
112 *incontinence*: lack of restraint.
113 *pleurisy*: here 'excess'.
131 *example*: precedent.

But mine. In mine my miseries are born.
I prithee, sorrow, leave a little room
In my confounded and tormented mind
For understanding to deliberate
The cause or author of this accident.
A close advantage of my absence made
To dispossess me both of land and wife –
And all the profit does arise to him
By whom my absence was first moved and urged.
These circumstances, uncle, tell me you
Are the suspected author of those wrongs,
Whereof the lightest is more heavy than
The strongest patience can endure to bear.

Exit CHARLEMONT.

SCENE II

Enter D'AMVILLE, SEBASTIAN *and* LANGUEBEAU SNUFF.

D'AMVILLE. Now, sir, your business?
SEBASTIAN. My annuity.
D'AMVILLE. Not a denier.
SEBASTIAN. How would you ha'me live?
D'AMVILLE. Why turn crier. Cannot you turn crier?
SEBASTIAN. Yes.
D'AMVILLE. Then do so: y'have a good voice for't.
Y'are excellent at crying of a rape.
SEBASTIAN. Sir, I confess in particular respect to yourself I was somewhat forgetful. General honesty possessed me.
D'AMVILLE. Go: th'art the base corruption of my blood
And like a tetter grow'st unto my flesh.
SEBASTIAN. Inflict any punishment upon me. The severity shall not discourage me, if it be not shameful,

---

138 *close*: secret.
141 *moved*: suggested.
2 *denier*: a French coin which was, by the sixteenth century, almost valueless.
3 *crier*: town-crier.
6 *in . . . yourself*: in respect due particularly to you (as my father).
10 *tetter*: rash.

so you'll but put money i'my purse. The want of money makes a free spirit more mad than the possession does an usurer.

D'AMVILLE. Not a farthing.

SEBASTIAN. Would you ha'me turn purse-taker? 'Tis the next way to do't. For want is like the rack: it draws a man to endanger himself to the gallows rather than endure it.

Enter CHARLEMONT. D'AMVILLE *counterfeits to take him for a ghost.*

D'AMVILLE. What art thou? Stay! Assist my troubled sense:
My apprehension will distract me. Stay!

LANGUEBEAU SNUFF *avoids him fearfully.*

SEBASTIAN. What art thou? Speak!

CHARLEMONT. The spirit of Charlemont.

D'AMVILLE. O stay! Compose me. I dissolve.

LANGUEBEAU. No, 'tis profane: spirits are invisible. 'Tis the fiend i'the likeness of Charlemont. I will have no conversation with Satan. *Exit* LANGUEBEAU.

SEBASTIAN. The spirit of Charlemont? I'll try that.

Strikes and the blow is returned.

'Fore God thou say'st true; th'art all spirit.

D'AMVILLE. Go call the officers. *Exit* D'AMVILLE.

CHARLEMONT. Th'art a villain, and the son of a villain.

SEBASTIAN. You lie.

Fight. SEBASTIAN *is down.*

CHARLEMONT. Have at thee.

Enter the ghost of MONTFERRERS.

Revenge, to thee I'll dedicate this work.

MONTFERRERS. Hold Charlemont!
Let him revenge my murder and thy wrongs
To whom the justice of revenge belongs.

Exit the ghost of MONTFERRERS.

CHARLEMONT. You torture me between the passion of

---

17 *purse-taker*: pickpocket.
20 s.d. *counterfeits*: pretends.
22 *distract*: drive mad.
25 *profane*: earthly.
29 *spirit*: lively courage.

my blood and the religion of my soul.

SEBASTIAN *rises.*

SEBASTIAN. A good, honest fellow.

Enter D'AMVILLE *with officers.*

D'AMVILLE. What? Wounded? Apprehend him. Sir, is this your salutation for the courtesy I did you when we parted last? You ha'forgot I lent you a thousand crowns. (*To officers*) First, let him answer for this riot. When the law is satisfied for that an action for his debt shall clap him up again. (*To Charlemont*) I took you for a spirit and I'll conjure you before I ha'done.

CHARLEMONT. No. I'll turn conjurer. Devil, within this circle, in the midst of all thy force and malice, I conjure thee do thy worst.

D'AMVILLE. Away with him.

Exeunt officers with CHARLEMONT.

SEBASTIAN. I have got a scratch or two here for your sake. I hope you'll give me money to pay the surgeon.

D'AMVILLE. Borachio! Fetch a thousand crowns. I am content to countenance the freedom of your spirit when 'tis worthily employed. A'God's name give behaviour the full scope of generous liberty, but let it not disperse and spend itself in courses of unbounded licence. Here, pay for your hurts. *Exit* D'AMVILLE.

SEBASTIAN. I thank you, sir . . . Generous liberty . . . That is to say, freely to bestow my abilities to honest purposes. Methinks I should not follow that instruction now if, having the means to do an honest office for an honest fellow, I should neglect it. Charlemont lies in prison for a thousand crowns. And here I have a thousand crowns. Honesty tells me 'twere well done to release Charlemont. But discretion says I had much ado to come by this, and when this shall be gone I

---

41 *Apprehend*: arrest.

46 *clap him up*: imprison.

50 *circle*: the circle is commonly associated with conjuring: Ribner quotes Cornelius Agrippa (1651): '. . . a circle being the largest and perfectest of all [geometrical figures] is judged to be the most fit for bondings and conjurations.'

55ff. As Borachio seems not to be on stage here, he must enter at D'Amville's call, exit for the money and return with it.

56 *countenance*: tolerate.

know not where to finger any more, especially if I employ it to this use, which is like to endanger me into my father's perpetual displeasure. And then I may go hang myself or be forced to do that will make another save me the labour. No matter. Charlemont, thou gav'st me my life and that's somewhat of a purer earth than gold, as fine as it is. 'Tis no courtesy I do thee, but thankfulness. I owe thee it and I'll pay it. He fought bravely, but the officers dragged him villainously. Arrant knaves for using him so discourteously: may the sins o'the poor folk be so few that you sha'not be able to spare so much out o'your gettings as will pay for the hire of a lame, starved hackney to ride to an execution but go afoot to the gallows and be hanged. May elder brothers turn good husbands and younger brothers get good wives, that there be no need of debt-books nor use of sergeants. May there be all peace but i'the war and all charity but i'the devil, so that prisons may be turned to hospitals though the officers live o'the benevolence. If this curse might come to pass the world would say 'Blessed be he that curseth'. *Exit.*

SCENE III

Enter CHARLEMONT *in prison.*

CHARLEMONT. I grant thee, heaven, thy goodness doth command
Our punishments, but yet no further than
The measure of our sins. How should they else
Be just? Or how should that good purpose of
Thy justice take effect by bounding men
Within the confines of humanity
When our afflictions do exceed our crimes?
Then they do rather teach the barb'rous world
Examples that extend her cruelties
Beyond their own dimensions, and instruct
Our actions to be more, more barbarous.
O my afflicted soul! How torment swells

82 *gettings*: earnings.
86 *sergeants*: here officials with power of arrest.
89 *benevolence*: alms, donations.
3 *measure*: amount.

Thy apprehension with profane conceit
Against the sacred justice of my God!
Our own constructions are the authors of
Our misery. We never measure our
Conditions but with men above us in
Estate, so while our spirits labour to
Be higher than our fortunes th'are more base.
Since all those attributes which make men seem
Superior to us are man's subjects and
Were made to serve him, the repining man
Is of a servile spirit to deject
The value of himself below their estimation.

Enter SEBASTIAN *with the keeper.*

SEBASTIAN. Here, take my sword. How now, my wild swaggerer? Y'are tame enough now, are you not? The penury of a prison is like a soft consumption – 'twill humble the pride o'your mortality and arm your soul in complete patience to endure the weight of affliction without feeling it. What, hast no music in thee? Th'hast trebles and basses enough: treble injury and base usage. But trebles and basses make poor music without means. Thou want'st means, dost? What, dost droop? Art dejected?

CHARLEMONT. No, sir, I have a heart above the reach
Of thy most violent maliciousness;
A fortitude in scorn of thy contempt
(Since fate is pleased to have me suffer it)
That can bear more than thou hast power t'inflict.
I was a baron. I've lost a signory
That was confined within a piece of earth,
A wart upon the body of the world.
But now I am an emp'ror of a world,
This little world of man. My passions are
My subjects, and I can command them laugh
Whilst thou dost tickle 'em to death with misery.

---

13 *profane conceit*: irreligious fancy.
15 *constructions*: interpretations.
27 *penury*: need, misery.
33 *means*: (a) the middle part in harmony; (b) means to live by (here specifically the money to get out of gaol).
40 *signory*: lordship.

SEBASTIAN. 'Tis bravely spoken and I love thee for't. Thou liest here for a thousand crowns. Here are a thousand to redeem thee. Not for the ransom o'my life thou gav'st me – that I value not at one crown. 'Tis none o'my deed: thank my father for't. 'Tis his goodness, yet he looks not for thanks for he does it underhand, out of a reserved disposition to do thee good without ostentation . . . Out o'great heart you'll refuse't now, will you?

CHARLEMONT. No. Since I must submit myself to fate I never will neglect the offer of one benefit but entertain them as her favours and th'inductions to some end of better fortune, as whose instrument I thank thy courtesy.

SEBASTIAN. Well, come along.

Exeunt CHARLEMONT, SEBASTIAN *and the keeper.*

SCENE IV

Enter D'AMVILLE *and* CASTABELLA.

D'AMVILLE. Daughter you did not well to urge me; I
Ha'done no more than justice. Charlemont
Shall die and rot in prison – and 'tis just.

CASTABELLA. O father, mercy is an attribute
As high as justice; an essential part
Of his unbounded goodness, whose divine
Impression, form and image man should bear.
And, methinks, man should love to imitate
His mercy, since the only countenance
Of justice were destruction if the sweet
And loving favour of his mercy did
Not mediate between it and our weakness.

D'AMVILLE. Forbear. You will displease me: he shall rot.

CASTABELLA. Dear sir, since by your greatness you
Are nearer heav'n in place, be nearer it
In goodness. Rich men should transcend the poor
As clouds the earth, raised by the comfort of
The sun to water dry and barren grounds.

---

49 *redeem*: repay a bond.
58 *inductions*: introductions.
9 *countenance*: manifestation.
12 *mediate*: act as intermediary.

If neither the impression in your soul
Of goodness, nor the duty of your place –
As goodness' substitute – can move you, then
Let nature, which in savages, in beasts,
Can stir to pity, tell you that he is
Your kinsman . . .

D'AMVILLE. You expose your honesty
To strange construction: why should you so urge
Release for Charlemont? Come, you profess
More nearness to him than your modesty
Can answer. You have tempted my suspicion.
I tell thee he shall starve and die and rot.

Enter CHARLEMONT *and* SEBASTIAN.

CHARLEMONT. Uncle, I thank you.

D'AMVILLE. (*aside*) Much good do it you . . . Who did release him?

SEBASTIAN. I.

Exit CASTABELLA.

D'AMVILLE. You are a villain.

SEBASTIAN. Y'are my father.

Exit SEBASTIAN.

D'AMVILLE. (*aside*) I must temporise . . .
Nephew, had not his open freedom made
My disposition known, I would ha'borne
The course and inclination of my love
According to the motion of the sun,
Invisibly enjoyed and understood.

CHARLEMONT. That shows your good works are directed to
No other end than goodness. I was rash
I must confess. But . . .

D'AMVILLE. I will excuse you.
To lose a father and, as you may think,
Be disinherited it must be granted
Are motives to impatience. But, for death,
Who can avoid it? And for his estate,
In the uncertainty of both your lives
'Twas done discreetly to confer't upon
A known successor, being the next in blood,
And one, dear nephew, whom in time to come
You shall have cause to thank. I will not be
Your dispossessor but your guardian;

I will supply your father's vacant place
To guide your green improvidence of youth
And make you ripe for your inheritance.
CHARLEMONT. Sir, I embrace your gen'rous promises.
They embrace.

Enter ROUSARD, *sick, and* CASTABELLA.

ROUSARD. Embracing? I behold the object that
Mine eye affects: dear cousin Charlemont!
D'AMVILLE. My elder son! He meets you happily,
For with the hand of our whole family
We interchange th'indenture of our loves.
CHARLEMONT. And I accept it, yet not joyfully,
Because y'are sick.
D'AMVILLE. Sir, his affection's sound
Though he be sick in body.
ROUSARD. Sick indeed.
A gen'ral weakness did surprise my health
The very day I married Castabella,
As if my sickness were a punishment
That did arrest me for some injury
I then committed. (*To Castabella*) Credit me, my love,
I pity thy ill fortune to be matched
With such a weak, unpleasing bedfellow.
CASTABELLA. Believe me, sir, it never troubles me:
I am as much respectless to enjoy
Such pleasure as ignorant what it is.
CHARLEMONT. (*aside*) Thy sex's wonder. Unhappy Charlemont.
D'AMVILLE. Come, let's to supper. There we will confirm
The eternal bond of our concluded love.
Exeunt all.

---

53 *green*: immature.
57 *affects*: loves.
60 *indenture*: formal pronouncement.
72 *respectless*: indifferent.

ACT IV

SCENE I

Enter CATAPLASMA *and* SOQUETTE *with needlework.*

CATAPLASMA. Come, Soquette, your work, let's examine your work. What's here? A medlar with a plum tree growing hard by it, the leaves o'the plum tree falling off, the gum issuing out o'the perished joints, and the branches some of 'em dead and some rotten, and yet but a young plum tree. In good sooth, very pretty.

SOQUETTE. The plum tree, forsooth, grows so near the medlar that the medlar sucks and draws all the sap from it and the natural strength o'the ground, so that it cannot prosper.

CATAPLASMA. How conceited you are! But here th'ast made a tree to bear no fruit. Why's that?

SOQUETTE. There grows a savin tree next it, forsooth.

CATAPLASMA. Forsooth, you are a little too witty in that.

Enter SEBASTIAN.

SEBASTIAN. But this honeysuckle winds about this whitethorn very prettily and lovingly, sweet mistress Cataplasma.

CATAPLASMA. Monsieur Sebastian! In good faith, very uprightly welcome this evening.

SEBASTIAN. What, moralising upon this gentlewoman's needlework? Let's see.

CATAPLASMA. No, sir. Only examining whether it be done to the true nature and life o'the thing.

SEBASTIAN. Here y'ave set a medlar with a bachelor's button o'one side and a snail o'th'tother. The

---

2 *medlar*: the medlar pear was often used to symbolise female genitalia.
plum tree: also sometimes used in the same way.

13 *savin*: the berries of this tree were often used to induce abortion.

20 *uprightly*: including sexual innuendo (erect penis).

bachelor's button should have held his head up more pertly towards the medlar; the snail, o'th'tother side, should ha'been wrought with an artificial laziness, doubling his tail and putting out his horn but half the length. And then the medlar, falling as it were from the lazy snail and inclining towards the pert bachelor's button, their branches spreading and winding one within another as if they did embrace. But here's a moral. A pop'ring pear tree growing upon the bank of a river, seeming continually to look downwards into the water as if it were enamoured of it, and ever as the fruit ripens lets it fall for love, as it were, into her lap; which the wanton stream, like a strumpet, no sooner receives but she carries it away and bestows it upon some other creature she maintains, still seeming to play and dally under the pop'ring so long that it has almost washed away the earth from the root, and now the poor tree stands as if it were ready to fall and perish by that whereon it spent all the substance it had.

CATAPLASMA. Moral for you that love those wanton running waters.

SEBASTIAN. But is not my lady Levidulcia come yet?

CATAPLASMA. Her purpose promised us her company ere this. Lirie, your lute and book.

SEBASTIAN. Well said. A lesson o'th'lute to entertain the time with till she comes.

CATAPLASMA. Sol, fa, mi, la . . . mi, mi, mi . . . Precious! Dost not see 'mi' between the two crotchets? Strike me full there . . . So . . . forward . . . This is a sweet strain and thou finger'st it beastly. 'Mi' is a large there

---

27 *bachelor's button*: lovers carried this flower, believing that so long as it stayed fresh so would their love affairs.
28 *snail*: symbol of sexual potency.
29 *artificial*: artistic.
35 *pop'ring pear tree*: the fruit of this tree was often used to refer to the male sex organs.
45 *spent*: carrying the sexual sense of ejaculation.
50 *Lirie*: It is possible, as Nicoll suggests, that the text is corrupt here. However, 'Lirie' may be a contraction of 'liripoop', used at this time to mean a smart or silly person, in which case the word is addressed playfully to Soquette.
56 *large*: a type of single note in the musical notation developed by Franco Cologne.

and the prick that stands before 'mi' a long; always halve your note . . . Now . . . Run your division pleasingly with those quavers. Observe all your graces i'the touch . . . Here's a sweet close . . . strike it full – it sets off your music delicately.

Enter LANGUEBEAU SNUFF *and* LEVIDULCIA.

LANGUEBEAU. Purity be in this house.

CATAPLASMA. 'Tis now entered, and welcome with your good ladyship.

SEBASTIAN. Cease that music. Here's sweeter instrument.

LEVIDULCIA. Restrain your liberty. See you not Snuff?

SEBASTIAN. What does the stinkard here? Put Snuff out – he's offensive.

LEVIDULCIA. No. The credit of his company defends my being abroad from the eye of suspicion.

CATAPLASMA. Will't please your ladyship go up into the closet? There are those falls and tires I told you of.

LEVIDULCIA. Monsieur Snuff, I shall request your patience. My stay will not be long.

Exit with SEBASTIAN.

LANGUEBEAU. My duty, madam . . . Falls and tires? I begin to suspect what falls and tires you mean: my lady and Sebastian the fall and the tire, and I but the shadow. I perceive the purity of my conversation is used but for a property to cover the uncleanness of their purposes. The very contemplation o'the thing makes the spirit of the flesh begin to wriggle in my blood. And here my desire has met with an object

---

57 *prick*: (a) a dot used in musical notation; (b) penis. The 'mi' of ll. 56–7 carries the obvious musical sense, but also = 'me' to convey the obscene sub-sense.

58 *division*: (a) a rapid passage of melody, dividing a series of long notes into short notes; (b) the opening of the legs.

59 *quavers*: (a) notes half as long as a crotchet; (b) sexual excitement.

60 *close*: (a) finale; (b) act of intercourse.

67 *stinkard*: smelly person.
Snuff: playing on the connection between Languebeau's name and the smell of a candle-end.

72 *falls and tires*: falls were veils, tires a type of hat: both words were used with overtones of sexual intercourse.

78 *shadow*: literally a border attached to a bonnet; figuratively an onlooker or cover for Levidulcia and Sebastian.

already. This gentlewoman, methinks, should be swayed with the motion, living in a house where moving example is so common. Temptation has prevailed over me and I will attempt to make it overcome her . . . Mistress Cataplasma – my lady, it seems, has some business that requires her stay. The fairness o'the evening invites me into the air: will it please you give this gentlewoman leave to leave her work and walk a turn or two with me for honest recreation?

CATAPLASMA. With all my heart, sir. Go, Soquette, give ear to his instructions: you may get understanding by his company, I can tell you.

LANGUEBEAU. In the way of holiness, mistress Cataplasma.

CATAPLASMA. Good monsieur Snuff. I will attend your return.

LANGUEBEAU. (*to Soquette*) Your hand, gentlewoman.
(*Aside*) The flesh is humble till the spirit move it,
But when 'tis raised it will command above it.

Exeunt all.

SCENE II

Enter D'AMVILLE, CHARLEMONT *and* BORACHIO.

D'AMVILLE. Your sadness and the sickness of my son
Have made our company and conference
Less free and pleasing than I purposed it.

CHARLEMONT. Sir, for the present I am much unfit
For conversation or society.
With pardon I will rudely take my leave.

D'AMVILLE. Good night, dear nephew.

Exit CHARLEMONT.

See'st thou that same man?

BORACHIO. Your meaning, sir?

D'AMVILLE. That fellow's life, Borachio,

---

84 *swayed . . . motion*: influenced by the prevailing sexual licence of the house.

6 *rudely*: abruptly.

Like a superfluous letter in the law,
Endangers our assurance.
BORACHIO. Scrape him out.
D'AMVILLE. Wou't do't?
BORACHIO. Give me your purpose, I will do it.
D'AMVILLE. Sad melancholy has drawn Charlemont
With meditation on his father's death
Into the solitary walk behind the church.
BORACHIO. The churchyard? This the fittest place for death.
Perhaps he's praying – then he's fit to die.
We'll send him charitably to his grave.
D'AMVILLE. No matter how thou tak'st him. First take this. *Gives* BORACHIO *a pistol.*
Thou know'st the place: observe his passages
And with the most advantage make a stand,
That, favoured by the darkness of the night,
His breast may fall upon thee at so near
A distance that he sha'not shun the blow.
The deed once done thou mayst retire with safety:
The place is unfrequented and his death
Will be imputed to th'attempt of thieves.
BORACHIO. Be careless. Let your mind be free and clear:
This pistol shall discharge you of your fear.
Exit BORACHIO.
D'AMVILLE. But let me call my projects to account,
For what effect and end I have engaged
Myself in all this blood. To leave a state
To the succession of my proper blood.
But how shall that succession be continued?
Not in my elder son I fear. Disease
And weakness have disabled him for issue.
For the tother his loose humour will endure

9–10 The idea is that a single letter in a legal document might alter the sense to a dangerous degree (an example, though not strictly a legal one, is the deliberate ambiguity of Mortimer's 'Edwardum occidere nolite timere bonum est' in Marlowe's *Edward II*, V.ii).

16–17 The idea echoes Hamlet's decision not to murder Claudius while he is apparently at prayer, for a praying man is in a state of grace and thus spiritually prepared to die.

20 *make a stand*: take up a position.

32 *proper*: own.

No bond of marriage – and I doubt his life,
His spirit is so boldly dangerous.
O pity that the profitable end
Of such a prosp'rous murder should be lost!
Nature forbid. I hope I have a body
That will not suffer me to lose my labour
For want of issue, yet. But then 't must be
A bastard. Tush, they only father bastards
That father other men's begettings. Daughter!
Be it mine own, let it come whence it will.
I am resolved. Daughter!

Enter servant.

SERVANT. My lord?
D'AMVILLE. I prithee call my daughter.

Enter CASTABELLA.

CASTABELLA. Your pleasure, sir?
D'AMVILLE. Is thy husband i'bed?
CASTABELLA. Yes my lord.
D'AMVILLE. The evening's fair. I prithee walk a turn or two.
CASTABELLA. Come, Jaspar.
D'AMVILLE. No.
We'll walk but to the corner o'the church,
And I have something to speak privately.
CASTABELLA. No matter, stay.

Exit servant.

D'AMVILLE. (*aside*) This falls out happily.

Exeunt D'AMVILLE *and* CASTABELLA.

SCENE III

Enter CHARLEMONT, BORACHIO *dogging him in the churchyard. The clock strikes twelve.*

CHARLEMONT. Twelve.
BORACHIO. 'Tis a good hour; 'twill strike one anon.

---

37 *doubt*: am afraid for.
60 *happily*: fortunately.
2 *'twill . . . anon*: Borachio puns (rather desperately) on the ideas of the clock striking one and of himself striking Charlemont.

CHARLEMONT. How fit a place for contemplation is this dead of night, among the dwellings of the dead . . . This grave . . . perhaps th'inhabitant was in his lifetime the possessor of his own desires. Yet in the midst of all his greatness and his wealth he was less rich and less contented than in this poor piece of earth, lower and lesser than a cottage. For here he neither wants nor cares: now that his body savours of corruption he enjoys a sweeter rest than e'er he did amongst the sweetest pleasures of this life. For here there's nothing troubles him . . . And there . . . in that grave lies another. He, perhaps, was in his life as full of misery as this of happiness: and here's an end of both. Now both their states are equal. O that man, with so much labour should aspire to worldly height, when in the humble earth the world's condition's at the best, or scorn inferior men, since to be lower than a worm is to be higher than a king!

BORACHIO. Then fall and rise!

Discharges; gives false fire.

CHARLEMONT. What villain's hand was that? Save thee or thou shalt perish.

They fight.

BORACHIO. Zounds, unsaved I think.

Falls.

CHARLEMONT. What, have I killed him? Whatsoe'er thou beest I would thy hand had prospered, for I was unfit to live and well prepared to die. What shall I do? Accuse myself, submit me to the law and that will quickly end this violent increase of misery. But 'tis a murder to be accessory to mine own death. I will not. I will take this opportunity to scape: it may be heav'n reserves me to some better end.

Exit CHARLEMONT.

Enter LANGUEBEAU *and* SOQUETTE *into the churchyard.*

SOQUETTE. Nay, good sir, I dare not. In good sooth I come of a generation, both by father and mother,

---

10 *savours*: smells.
21 s.d. *Discharges . . .* : i.e. misfires.

that were all as fruitful as costard-mongers' wives.

LANGUEBEAU. Tush, then a tympany is the greatest danger can be feared. Their fruitfulness turns but to a certain kind of phlegmatic windy disease.

SOQUETTE. I must put my understanding to your trust, sir. I would be loath to be deceived.

LANGUEBEAU. No, conceive, thou sha'not. Yet thou shalt profit by my instruction too. My body is not every day drawn dry, wench.

SOQUETTE. Yet methinks, sir, your want of use should rather make your body like a well: the lesser 'tis drawn the sooner it grows dry.

LANGUEBEAU. Thou shalt try that instantly.

SOQUETTE. But we want place and opportunity.

LANGUEBEAU. We have both. This is the backside of the house which the superstitious call Saint Winifred's church and is verily a convenient, unfrequented place, Where under the close curtains of the night;

SOQUETTE. You purpose i'the dark to make me light.

SNUFF *pulls out a sheet, a hair and a beard.*

But what ha'you there?

LANGUEBEAU. This disguise is for security sake, wench. There's a talk, thou know'st, that the ghost of old Montferrers walks: in this church he was buried. Now, if any stranger fall upon us before our business be ended, in this disguise I shall be taken for that ghost and never be called to examination, I warrant thee. Thus we shall scape both prevention and discovery. How do I look in this habit, wench?

SOQUETTE. So like a ghost that notwithstanding I have some foreknowledge of you you make my hair stand almost on end.

LANGUEBEAU. I will try how I can kiss in this beard. O,

---

35 *costard-mongers*: see Textual note, p. 197.
36 *tympany*: swelling (here 'pregnancy' and 'swollen by wind').
38 *phlegmatic*: see above, p. 000 n.; phlegm was largely composed of water.
39 *understanding*: with the sexual overtone of 'lying beneath'.
41 *conceive*: (a) believe me; (b) get pregnant.
42–6 Playing on the proverb 'Drawn wells are seldom dry.'
53 *light*: i.e. a whore.
53 s.d. *hair*: wig.
62 *habit*: outfit.
65 *on*: see Textual note, p. 197.

fie, fie, fie, I will put it off and then kiss and then put it on. I can do the rest without kissing.

Enter CHARLEMONT *doubtfully with his sword drawn; is upon them before they are aware. They run divers ways and leave the disguise.*

CHARLEMONT. What ha'we here? A sheet, a hair, a beard? What end was this disguise intended for? No matter what – I'll not expostulate the purpose of a friendly accident. Perhaps it may accommodate my scape. I fear I am pursued: for more assurance I'll hide me here i'th'charnel house, this convocation-house of dead men's skulls.

To get into the charnel house he takes hold of a death's head; it slips and staggers him.

Death's head? Deceiv'st my hold? Such is the trust to all mortality.

Hides himself in the charnel house.

Enter D'AMVILLE *and* CASTABELLA.

CASTABELLA. My lord, the night grows late. Your lordship spake of something you desired to move in private.

D'AMVILLE. Yes, now I'll speak it. The argument is love. The smallest ornament of thy sweet form (that abstract of all pleasure) can command the senses into passion, and thy entire perfection is my object. Yet I love thee with the freedom of my reason: I can give thee reason for my love.

CASTABELLA. Love me, my lord? I do believe it, for I am the wife of him you love.

D'AMVILLE. 'Tis true. By my persuasion thou wert forced to marry one unable to perform the office of a husband. I was the author of the wrong. My conscience suffers under't, and I would disburden it by satisfaction.

---

68 s.d. *doubtfully*: fearfully.
71 *expostulate*: question.
74 *convocation-house*: meeting-place.
79 *move*: speak of.
82 *abstract*: quintessence.
92 *satisfaction*: adequate repayment.

CASTABELLA. How?

D'AMVILLE. I will supply that pleasure to thee which he cannot.

CASTABELLA. Are y'a devil or a man?

D'AMVILLE. A man, and such a man as can return thy entertainment with as prodigal a body as the covetous desire of woman ever was delighted with, so that besides the full performance of thy empty husband's duty thou shalt have the joy of children to continue the succession of thy blood. For the appetite that steals her pleasure draws the forces of the body to an united strength and puts 'em altogether into action, never fails of procreation. All the purposes of man aim but at one of these two ends, pleasure or profit; and in this one sweet conjunction of our loves they both will meet. Would it not grieve thee that a stranger to thy blood should lay the first foundation of his house upon the ruins of thy family?

CASTABELLA. Now heaven defend me! May my memory be utterly extinguished and the heir of him that was my father's enemy raise his eternal monument upon our ruins, ere the greatest pleasure or the greatest profit ever tempt me to continue it by incest.

D'AMVILLE. Incest? Tush, these distances affinity observes are articles of bondage cast upon our freedoms by our own subjections. Nature allows a gen'ral liberty of generation to all creatures else. Shall man, to whose command and use all creatures were made subject, be less free than they?

CASTABELLA. O God! Is thy unlimited and infinite omnipotence less free because thou dost no ill? Or, if you argue merely out of nature do you not degenerate from that, and are you not unworthy the prerogative of nature's masterpiece when basely you prescribe yourself authority and law from their examples whom you should command? I could confute you, but the horror of the argument confounds my understanding. Sir, I know you do but try me in your son's behalf, suspecting that my strength and youth of blood cannot contain themselves with impotence. Believe me,

---

99 *prodigal*: lavish in giving.
119 *subjections*: submissions.

sir, I never wronged him. If it be your lust, O quench it on their prostituted flesh whose trade of sin can please desire with more delight and less offence. The poison of your breath, evaporated from so foul a soul, infects the air more than the damps that rise from bodies.

D'AMVILLE. Kiss me: I warrant thee my breath is sweet. These dead men's bones lie here of purpose to invite us to supply the number of the living. Come we'll get young bones and do't. I will enjoy thee. No? Nay then invoke your great supposed protector. I will do't.

CASTABELLA. Supposed protector? Are y'an atheist? Then I know my prayers and tears are spent in vain. O patient heaven, why dost thou not express thy wrath in thunderbolts to tear the frame of man in pieces? How can earth endure the burden of this wickedness without an earthquake, or the angry face of heaven be not inflamed with lightning?

D'AMVILLE. Conjure up the devil and his dam, cry to the graves: the dead can hear thee – invocate their help.

CASTABELLA. O, would this grave might open and my body were bound to the dead carcass of a man forever, ere it entertain the lust of this detested villain.

D'AMVILLE. Tereus-like, thus I will force my passage to . . .

CHARLEMONT rises in the disguise and frights D'AMVILLE away.

CHARLEMONT. The devil! . . . Now lady, with the hand of Charlemont I thus redeem you from the arm of lust . . . My Castabella!

CASTABELLA. My dear Charlemont!

CHARLEMONT. For all my wrongs I thank thee, gracious heaven; th'ast made me satisfaction to reserve me for this blessed purpose. Now, sweet death, I'll bid thee welcome. Come, I'll guard thee home and then I'll cast myself into the arms of apprehension that the law may make this worthy work the crown of all my actions, being the best and last.

---

138 *damps*: poisonous vapours.
153 *invocate*: call upon.
157 *Tereus*: in Greek myth Tereus raped and mutilated Philomela.
167 *apprehension*: arrest.

CASTABELLA. The last? The law? Now heaven forbid, what ha'you done?

CHARLEMONT. Why, I have killed a man – not murdered him, my Castabella: he would ha'murdered me.

CASTABELLA. Then, Charlemont, the hand of heaven directed thy defence . . . That wicked atheist, I suspect his plot.

CHARLEMONT. My life he seeks. I would he had it since he has deprived me of those blessings that should make me love it. Come, I'll give it him.

CASTABELLA. You sha'not. I will first expose myself to certain danger than for my defence destroy the man that saved me from destruction.

CHARLEMONT. Thou canst not satisfy me better than to be the instrument of my release from misery.

CASTABELLA. Then work it by escape. Leave me to this protection that still guards the innocent, or I will be a partner in your destiny.

CHARLEMONT. My soul is heavy. Come, lie down to rest;
These are the pillows whereon men sleep best.

They lie down with either of them a death's head for a pillow.

Enter LANGUEBEAU *seeking* SOQUETTE.

LANGUEBEAU. Soquette! Soquette! Soquette! O, art thou there?

He mistakes the body of BORACHIO *for* SOQUETTE.

Verily thou liest in a fine premeditate readiness for the purpose . . . Come, kiss me sweet Soquette . . . Now purity defend me from the sin of Sodom . . . This is a creature of the masculine gender . . . Verily the man is blasted . . . Yea? Cold and stiff? . . . Murder, murder, murder! *Exit* LANGUEBEAU.

Enter D'AMVILLE *distractedly; starts at the sight of a death's head.*

D'AMVILLE. Why dost thou stare upon me? Thou art not the skull of him I murdered. What has thou to do to vex my conscience? Sure thou wert the head of a most

192 *premeditate*: thought out in advance.
198ff. See Textual note, p. 197.

dogged usurer, th'art so uncharitable. And that bawd, the sky there, she could shut the windows and the doors of this great chamber of the world, and draw the curtains of the clouds between those lights and me about this bed of earth, when that same strumpet Murder and myself committed sin together. Then she could leave us i'the dark till the close deed was done; but now that I begin to feel the loathsome horror of my sin and (like a lecher emptied of his lust) desire to bury my face under my eye-brows and would steal from my shame unseen, she meets me i'the face with all her light-corrupted eyes to challenge payment o'me . . . O behold, yonder's the ghost of old Montferrers in a long white sheet, climbing yond' lofty mountain to complain to heaven of me . . . Montferrers! Pox o'fearfulness: 'tis nothing but a fair white cloud. Why, was I born a coward? He lies that says so. Yet the count'nance of a bloodless worm might ha'the courage now to turn my blood to water. The trembling motion of an aspen leaf would make me, like the shadow of that leaf, lie shaking under't. I could now commit a murder, were it but to drink the fresh, warm blood of him I murdered to supply the want and weakness o'mine own, 'tis grown so cold and phlegmatic.

LANGUEBEAU. (*within*) Murder, murder, murder!

D'AMVILLE. Mountains o'erwhelm me; the ghost of old Montferrers haunts me.

LANGUEBEAU. Murder, murder, murder!

D'AMVILLE. O, were my body circumvolved within that cloud, that when the thunder tears his passage open it might scatter me to nothing in the air.

Enter LANGUEBEAU SNUFF *with the watch.*

LANGUEBEAU. Here you shall find the murdered body.

D'AMVILLE. Black Beelzebub and all his hell-hounds come to apprehend me?

---

201 *dogged*: mean, malicious.
207 *close*: private, secret.
224 *phlegmatic*: see above, p. 000 n.
226 *Mountains o'erwhelm me*: see *Revelation* 6:16;
229f. Compare Faustus's dying speech in Marlowe's play. *circumvolved*: enveloped.

LANGUEBEAU. No, my good lord. We come to apprehend the murderer.

D'AMVILLE. The ghost, great Pluto, was a fool, unfit to be employed in any serious business for the state of hell. Why could not he ha'suffered me to raise the mountain o'my sins with one as damnable as all the rest and then ha'tumbled me to ruin? But apprehend me e'en between the purpose and the act, before it was committed!

WATCH. Is this the murderer? He speaks suspiciously.

LANGUEBEAU. No, verily. This is my lord D'Amville, and his distraction, I think, grows out of his grief for the loss of a faithful servant. For surely I take him to be Borachio that is slain.

D'AMVILLE. Ha! Borachio slain? Thou look'st like Snuff dost not?

LANGUEBEAU. Yes, in sincerity, my lord.

D'AMVILLE. Hark thee. Sawest thou not a ghost?

LANGUEBEAU. A ghost? Where my lord? . . . I smell a fox.

D'AMVILLE. Here i'the churchyard.

LANGUEBEAU. Tush, tush, their walking spirits are mere imaginary fables. There's no such thing in *rerum natura.* Here is a man slain, and with the spirit of consideration I rather think him to be the murderer got into that disguise than any such fantastic toy.

D'AMVILLE. My brains begin to put themselves in order. I apprehend thee now . . . 'Tis e'en so . . . Borachio! I will search the centre but I'll find the murderer.

WATCH. Here, here, here!

D'AMVILLE. Stay. Asleep? So soundly and so sweetly upon death's heads, and in a place so full of fear and horror? Sure there is some other happiness within the

---

235–43 See Textual note p. 197.

237 *Pluto*: in Greek mythology Pluto is a synonym for Hades/Hell.

253 *smell a fox*: i.e. am suspicious.

256–7 *in rerum natura*: among the things of nature. Ribner sees an allusion to Lucretius's *De Rerum Natura*, adding that the period saw that book as a 'virtual handbook of atheism' (p. 92). This is possible but seems inappropriate to Languebeau.

259 *toy*: trifle.

262 *centre*: i.e. of the earth.

freedom of the conscience than my knowledge e'er
attained to . . . Ho, ho, ho!
CHARLEMONT. Y'are welcome, uncle. Had you sooner
come
You had been sooner welcome. I'm the man
You seek: you sha'not need examine me.
D'AMVILLE. My nephew and my daughter! O my dear
Lamented blood, what fate has cast you thus
Unhappily upon this accident?
CHARLEMONT. You know, sir, she's as clear as chastity.
D'AMVILLE. As her own chastity: the time, the place,
All circumstances argue that unclear.
CASTABELLA. Sir, I confess it, and repentantly
Will undergo the selfsame punishment
That justice shall inflict on Charlemont.
CHARLEMONT. Unjustly she betrays her innocence.
WATCH. But, sir, she's taken with you and she must
To prison with you.
D'AMVILLE. There's no remedy.
Yet were it not my son's bed she abused,
My land should fly but both should be excused.
Exeunt all.

SCENE IV

Enter BELFOREST *and a servant.*

BELFOREST. Is not my wife come in yet?
SERVANT. No, my lord.
BELFOREST. Methinks she's very affectedly inclined
To young Sebastian's company o'late,
But jealousy is such a torment that
I am afraid to entertain it. Yet
The more I shun by circumstance to meet
Directly with it, the more I find
To circumvent my apprehension. First,
I know sh'as a perpetual appetite,
Which being so oft encountered with a man
Of such a bold, luxurious freedom as

271 *examine*: cross-examine, question.
2 *affectedly*: affectionately.
6 *by circumstance*: by indirect action.
11 *luxurious*: lecherous.

Sebastian is, and of so promising
A body, her own blood, corrupted, will
Betray her to temptation . . .

Enter FRESCO *closely.*

FRESCO. (*aside*) 'Precious! I was sent by his lady to see if her lord were in bed. I should ha'done't slyly without discovery, and now I am blurted upon 'em before I was aware. *Exit* FRESCO.

BELFOREST. Know you not the gentlewoman my wife brought home?

SERVANT. By sight, my lord. Her man was here but now.

BELFOREST. Her man? I prithee run and call him quickly . . .

Exit servant.

This villain, I suspect him ever since I found him hid behind the tapestry . . .

Enter FRESCO *and servant.*

Fresco! Th'art welcome, Fresco . . . Leave us.

Exit servant.

Dost hear, Fresco, is not my wife at thy mistress'?

FRESCO. I know not, my lord.

BELFOREST. I prithee tell me, Fresco. We are private. Tell me. Is not thy mistress a good wench?

FRESCO. How means your lordship that? A wench o'the trade?

BELFOREST. Yes, faith, Fresco, e'en a wench o'the trade.

FRESCO. O no, my lord. Those falling diseases cause baldness and my mistress recovers the loss of hair for she is a periwig maker.

BELFOREST. And nothing else?

FRESCO. Sells falls and tires and bodies for ladies, or so.

BELFOREST. So, sir: and she helps my lady to falls and bodies now and then, does she not?

FRESCO. At her ladyship's pleasure, my lord.

---

14 s.d. *closely*: quietly.
17 *blurted*: stumbled.
31–2 *wench o'the trade*: bawd and/or prostitute.
34 *falling diseases*: syphilis.
38 *falls and tires*: see above p. 000.
bodies: bodices, but also human bodies as prostitutes.

BELFOREST. Her pleasure, you rogue? You are the pandar to her pleasure, you varlet, are you not? You know the conveyances between Sebastian and my wife. Tell me the truth or by this hand I'll nail thy bosom to the earth. Stir not, you dog, but quickly tell the truth.

FRESCO. O yes! *Speaks like a crier.*

BELFOREST. Is not thy mistress a bawd to my wife?

FRESCO. O yes!

BELFOREST. And acquainted with her tricks and her plots and her devices?

FRESCO. O yes! If any man, court, city, or country, has found my lady Levidulcia in bed but my lord Belforest it is Sebastian.

BELFOREST. What, dost thou proclaim it? Dost thou cry it, thou villain?

FRESCO. Can you laugh it, my lord? I thought you meant to proclaim yourself cuckold.

Enter the watch.

BELFOREST. The watch? Met with my wish. I must request th'assistance of your offices.

FRESCO *runs away.*

'Sdeath, stay that villain. Pursue him.

Exeunt BELFOREST *and the watch.*

SCENE V

Enter LANGUEBEAU *importuning* SOQUETTE.

SOQUETTE. Nay, if you get me any more into the churchyard . . .

LANGUEBEAU. Why, Soquette, I never got thee there yet.

SOQUETTE. Got me there? No, not with child.

LANGUEBEAU. I promised thee I would not and I was as good as my word.

SOQUETTE. Yet your word was better then than your deed. But steal up into the little matted chamber o'the left hand.

LANGUEBEAU. I prithee let it be the right hand: thou left'st me before and I did not like that.

---

44 *conveyances*: contacts.
61 *'Sdeath*: On God's death.
3 *got thee*: had you sexually.

SOQUETTE. 'Precious, quickly. So soon as my mistress shall be in bed I'll come to you.

Exit LANGUEBEAU.

Enter SEBASTIAN, LEVIDULCIA *and* CATAPLASMA.

CATAPLASMA. I wonder Fresco stays so long.

SEBASTIAN. Mistress Soquette, a word with you.

They whisper.

LEVIDULCIA. If he brings word my husband is i'bed I will adventure one night's liberty to lie abroad . . . My strange affection to this man . . . 'Tis like that natural sympathy which e'en among the senseless creatures of the earth commands a mutual inclination and consent, for though it seems to be the free effect of mine own voluntary love, yet I can neither restrain it nor give reason for't. But now 'tis done, and in your power it lies to save my honour or dishonour me.

CATAPLASMA. Enjoy your pleasure, madam, without fear. I never will betray the trust you have committed to me, and you wrong yourself to let consideration of the sin molest your conscience. Methinks 'tis unjust that a reproach should be inflicted on a woman for offending but with one, when 'tis a light offence in husbands to commit with many.

LEVIDULCIA. So it seems to me . . . Why, how now, Sebastian? Making love to that gentlewoman? How many mistresses ha'you i'faith?

SEBASTIAN. In faith, none, for I think none of 'em are faithful; but otherwise as many as clean shirts. The love of a woman is like a mushroom; it grows in one night and will serve somewhat pleasingly next morning to breakfast, but afterwards waxes fulsome and unwholesome.

CATAPLASMA. Nay, by Saint Winifred, a woman's love lasts as long as winter fruit.

SEBASTIAN. 'Tis true: till new come in – by my experience no longer.

Enter FRESCO *running.*

---

39 *fulsome*: nauseous.

42 *winter fruit*: preserved or late fruit (which does not last long).

FRESCO. Somebody's doing has undone us and we are like pay dearly for't.

SEBASTIAN. Pay dear for what?

FRESCO. Will't not be a chargeable reckoning, think you, when here are half a dozen fellows coming to call us to account, with every man a several bill in his hand that we are not able to discharge?

Knock at the door.

CATAPLASMA. Passion o'me! What bouncing's that? Madam, withdraw yourself.

LEVIDULCIA. Sebastian, if you love me, save my honour.

Exeunt all except SEBASTIAN.

SEBASTIAN. What violence is this? What seek you? Zounds, you shall not pass!

Enter BELFOREST *and the watch.*

BELFOREST. Pursue the strumpet!

Exit watch.

Villain give me way or I will make my passage through thy blood.

SEBASTIAN. My blood would make it slippery, my lord. 'Twere better you would take another way: you may hap fall else.

They fight. Both slain.

I ha't i'faith SEBASTIAN *falls first. Dies.*

While BELFOREST *is staggering, enter* LEVIDULCIA.

LEVIDULCIA. O God! My husband, my Sebastian, husband! Neither can speak, yet both report my shame. Is this the saving of my honour, when their blood runs out in rivers and my lust the fountain whence it flows? Dear husband, let not thy departed spirit be displeased if with adult'rate lips I kiss thy cheek. Here I behold the hatefulness of lust, which brings me kneeling to embrace him dead, whose body living I did loath to touch. Now I can weep, but what can tears do good? When I weep only water they weep blood. But could

---

50 *bill*: (a) written document demanding payment; (b) weapon.
51 *discharge*: pay.
52 *bouncing*: knocking.
62 *hap*: happen to, perhaps.

I make an ocean with my tears, that on the flood this broken vessel of my body, laden heavy with light lust, might suffer shipwrack and so drown my shame: then weeping were to purpose. But, alas, the sea wants water enough to wash away the foulness of my name. O, in their wounds I feel my honour wounded to the death. Shall I outlive my honour? Must my life be made the world's example? Since it must, then thus in detestation of my deed, to make th'example move more forcibly to virtue, thus I seal it with a death as full of horror as my life of sin.

Stabs herself.

Enter the watch with CATAPLASMA, FRESCO, LANGUEBEAU SNUFF *and* SOQUETTE.

WATCH. Hold, madam! Lord, what a strange night is this.

LANGUEBEAU. May not Snuff be suffered to go out of himself?

WATCH. Nor you, nor any. All must go with us.
O, with what virtue lust should be withstood,
Since 'tis a fire quenched seldom without blood.

Exeunt all.

ACT V

SCENE I

Music. A closet discovered. A servant sleeping with lights and money before him.

D'AMVILLE. What, sleep'st thou?
SERVANT. No, my lord. Nor sleep nor wake.
But in a slumber troublesome to both.
D'AMVILLE. Whence comes this gold?
SERVANT. 'Tis part of the revénue
Due to your lordship since your brother's death.
D'AMVILLE. To bed. Leave me my gold.

---

86 Snuff puns on his own name.
V.i. s.d. *discovered*: revealed.

SERVANT. And me my rest.
Two things wherewith one man is seldom blessed.

Exit servant.

D'AMVILLE. Cease that harsh music. W'are not pleased with it.

He handles the gold.

Here sounds a music whose melodious touch
Like angels' voices ravishes the sense.
Behold thou ignorant astronomer,
Whose wand'ring speculation seeks among
The planets for men's fortunes, with amazement
Behold thine error and be planet-struck.
These are the stars whose operations make
The fortunes and the destinies of men.
Yond' lesser eyes of heaven, like subjects raised
Into their lofty houses when their prince
Rides underneath th'ambition of their loves,
Are mounted only to behold the face
Of your more rich imperious eminence
With unprevented sight. Unmask, fair queen:

Unpurses the gold.

Vouchsafe their expectations may enjoy
The gracious favour they admire to see;
These are the stars, the ministers of fate,
And man's high wisdom the superior power
To which their forces are subordinate.

Sleeps.

Enter the ghost of MONTFERRERS.

MONTFERRERS. D'Amville, with all thy wisdom th'art a fool:
Not like those fools that we term innocents,
But a most wretched, miserable fool,
Which instantly, to the confusion of
Thy projects, with despair thou shalt behold.

Exit ghost.

---

13 *planet-struck*: be struck by the power of gold (as men were thought to be influenced by the planets).

21 *unprevented*: unhindered.

22 *Vouchsafe*: permit that.

23 *admire*: wonder.

28 *innocents*: children and mental defectives.

D'AMVILLE *starts up.*

D'AMVILLE. What foolish dream dares interrupt my rest
To my confusion? How can that be since
My purposes have hitherto been borne
With prosp'rous judgement to secure success,
Which nothing lives to dispossess me of
But apprehended Charlemont? And him
This brain has made the happy instrument
To free suspicion, to annihilate
All interest and title of his own,
To seal up my assurance and confirm
My absolute possession by the law.
Thus while the simple, honest worshipper
Of a fantastic providence groans under
The burden of neglected misery,
My real wisdom has raised up a state
That shall eternise my posterity.

Enter servants with the body of Sebastian.

What's that?

SERVANT. The body of your younger son, slain by the lord Belforest.

D'AMVILLE. Slain? You lie . . . Sebastian, speak, Sebastian! H'as lost his hearing. A physician presently: go, call a surgeon.

ROUSARD. (*within*) Oh!

D'AMVILLE. What groan was that? How does my elder son? The sound came from his chamber.

SERVANT. He went sick to bed, my lord.

ROUSARD. (*within*) Oh!

D'AMVILLE. The cries of mandrakes never touched the ear
With more sad horror than that voice does mine.

Enter a servant running.

SERVANT. If ever you will see your son alive . . .

D'AMVILLE. Nature forbid I e'er should see him dead.

A bed drawn forth with ROUSARD.

Withdraw the curtains. O, how does my son?

SERVANT. Methinks he's ready to give up the ghost.

D'AMVILLE. Destruction take thee and thy fatal tongue.

---

52 *presently*: immediately.
59 *cries of mandrakes*: the mandrake plant was believed to shriek when pulled from the ground.

Death, where's the doctor? . . . Art not thou the face of that prodigious apparition stared upon me in my dream?

SERVANT. The doctor's come, my lord.

Enter doctor.

D'AMVILLE. Doctor, behold two patients, in whose cure thy skill may purchase an eternal fame. If thou hast any reading in Hippocrates, Galen or Avicen, if herbs, or drugs, or minerals have any power to save, now let thy practice and their sovereign use raise thee to wealth and honour.

DOCTOR. If any root of life remains within 'em capable of physic, fear 'em not, my lord.

ROUSARD. Oh!

D'AMVILLE. His gasping sighs are like the falling noise of some great building when the groundwork breaks. On these two pillars stood the stately frame and architecture of my lofty house. An earthquake shakes 'em, the foundation shrinks. Dear nature, in whose honour I have raised a work of glory to posterity, O bury not the pride of that great action under the fall and ruin of itself.

DOCTOR. My lord, these bodies are deprived of all the radical ability of nature. The heat of life is utterly extinguished. Nothing remains within the power of man that can restore them.

D'AMVILLE. Take this gold, extract the spirit of it and inspire new life into their bodies.

DOCTOR. Nothing can, my lord.

D'AMVILLE. You ha'not yet examined the true state and constitution of their bodies. Sure, you ha'not. I'll reserve their waters till the morning. Questionless their urines will inform you better.

---

72 *Hippocrates*: Greek physician, born on Cos *c.* 460 B.C.
Galen: (*c.* A.D. 129–99), born at Pergamum – with Hippocrates, taken as the ultimate authority on medicine.
Avicen: (or Avicenna) Arab physician; prolific writer on medicine.

88 *radical*: relating to that essential moisture in all living things without which, according to medieval thought, life could not be sustained.

DOCTOR. Ha, ha, ha!

D'AMVILLE. Dost laugh, thou villain? Must my wisdom, that has been the object of men's admiration, now become the subject of thy laughter?

ROUSARD. Oh! *Dies.*

ALL. He's dead.

D'AMVILLE. O, there expires the date of my posterity. Can nature be so simple or malicious to destroy the reputation of her proper memory? She cannot. Sure there is some power above her that controls her force.

DOCTOR. A power above nature? Doubt you that my lord? Consider but whence man receives his body and his form: not from corruption, like some worms and flies, but only from the generation of a man. For nature never did bring forth a man without a man, nor could the first man – being but the passive subject, not the active mover – be the maker of himself. So of necessity there must be a superior power to nature.

D'AMVILLE. Now to myself I am ridiculous. Nature, thou art a traitor to my soul; thou hast abused my trust. I will complain to a superior court: to right my wrong I'll prove thee a forger of false assurances. In yond Star Chamber thou shalt answer it. Withdraw the bodies. O, the sense of death begins to trouble my distracted soul.

SCENE II

Enter judges and officers.

1 JUDGE. Bring forth the malefactors to the bar.

Enter CATAPLASMA, SOQUETTE *and* FRESCO.

Are you the gentlewoman in whose house
The murders were committed?

CATAPLASMA. Yes, my lord.

---

104 *date*: period.
106 *proper*: own.
110–11 *corruption . . . flies*: it was believed that certain insects and reptiles were born from corrupt matter.
120 *Star Chamber*: (a) the heavens; (b) the court of Star Chamber where appeals from the Chancery Court were heard.
121 *sense*: awareness.

1 JUDGE. That worthy attribute of gentry, which
Your habit draws from ignorant respect,
Your name deserves not, nor yourself the name
Of woman since you are the poison that
Infects the honour of all womanhood.

CATAPLASMA. My lord, I am a gentlewoman, yet I must confess my poverty compels my life to a condition lower than my birth or breeding.

2 JUDGE. Tush, we know your birth.

1 JUDGE. But under colour to profess the sale
Of tires and toys for gentlewomen's pride,
You draw a frequentation of men's wives
To your licentious house, and there abuse
Their husbands.

FRESCO. Good my lord, her rent is great. The good gentlewoman has no other thing to live by but her lodgings, so she's forced to let her forerooms out to others and herself contented to lie backwards.

2 JUDGE. So.

1 JUDGE. Here is no evidence accuses you
For accessories to the murder, yet –
Since, from the spring of lust which you preserved
And nourished, ran th'effusion of that blood –
Your punishment shall come as near to death
As life can bear it. Law cannot inflict
Too much severity upon the cause
Of such abhorred effects.

2 JUDGE. Receive your sentence:
Your goods, since they were gotten by that means
Which brings diseases, shall be turned to th'use
Of hospitals; you carted through the streets
According to the common shame of strumpets,
Your bodies whipped till with the loss of blood
You faint under the hand of punishment.
Then, that the necessary force of want
May not provoke you to your former life,

---

5 *habit*: dress.
ignorant respect: the respect of ignorant people.
13 *under colour*: with the pretence of.
14 *toys*: trifles.
21 *lie backwards*: (a) use the back rooms; (b) prostitute herself.
26 *effusion*: pouring out.

You shall be set to painful labour, whose
Penurious gains shall only give you food
To hold up nature, mortify your flesh,
And make you fit for a repentant end.

ALL. O, good my lord!

1 JUDGE. No more. Away with 'em.

Exeunt CATAPLASMA, SOQUETTE, FRESCO.

Enter LANGUEBEAU SNUFF.

2 JUDGE. Now, monsieur Snuff! A man of your profession found in a place of such impiety!

LANGUEBEAU. I grant you, the place is full of impurity: so much the more need of instruction and reform. The purpose that carried me thither was with the spirit of conversion to purify their uncleanness, and I hope your lordship will say the law cannot take hold o'me for that.

1 JUDGE. No, sir, it cannot – but yet give me leave
To tell you that I hold your wary answer
Rather premeditated for excuse
Than spoken out of a religious purpose.
Where took you your degrees of scholarship?

LANGUEBEAU. I am no scholar, my lord. To speak the sincere truth I am Snuff the tallow chandler.

2 JUDGE. How comes your habit to be altered thus?

LANGUEBEAU. My lord Belforest, taking a delight in the cleanness of my conversation, withdrew me from that unclean life and put me in a garment fit for his society and my present profession.

1 JUDGE. His lordship did but paint a rotten post,
Or cover foulness fairly. Monsieur Snuff,
Back to your candle-making. You may give
The world more light with that than either with
Instruction or th'example of your life.

LANGUEBEAU. Thus the Snuff is put out.

Exit LANGUEBEAU.

---

40 *Penurious*: meagre.

58 Snuff's name now accurately designates his profession. The line also satirically touches on the fact that Puritan preachers were often of humble origin and limited formal education.

59 *habit*: dress.

69 the usual play on name and object.

Enter D'AMVILLE *distractedly, with the hearses of his sons borne after him.*

D'AMVILLE. Judgement, judgement!

2 JUDGE. Judgement, my lord? In what?

D'AMVILLE. Your judgements must resolve me in a case. Bring in the bodies. Nay, I will ha't tried. This is my case, my lord. My providence, ev'n in a moment, by the only hurt of one or two or three at most – and those put quickly out o'pain too, mark me. I had wisely raised a competent estate to my posterity – and is there not more wisdom and more charity in that, than for your lordship or your father or your grandsire to prolong the torment and the rack of rent from age to age upon your poor, penurious tenants? Yet, perhaps, without a penny profit to your heir. Is't not more wise, more charitable? Speak.

1 JUDGE. He is distracted.

D'AMVILLE. How? Distracted? Then you ha'no judgement. I can give you sense and solid reason for the very least distinguishable syllable I speak. Since my thrift was more charitable, more judicious than your grandsire's, why, I would fain know why your lordship lives to make a second generation from your father and the whole fry of my posterity extinguished in a moment. Not a brat left to succeed me. I would fain know that.

2 JUDGE. Grief for his children's death distempers him.

1 JUDGE. My lord, we will resolve you of your question.
In the meantime vouchsafe your place with us.

D'AMVILLE. I am contented, so you will resolve me.

Ascends.

Enter CHARLEMONT *and* CASTABELLA.

2 JUDGE. Now, monsieur Charlemont, you are accused
Of having murdered one Borachio that
Was servant to my lord D'Amville. How can
You clear yourself? Guilty or not guilty?

---

74 *providence*: prudence in providing for my successors.
77 *competent*: adequate.
80 *rack of rent*: 'Rack-rent was rent equal to or close to the actual value of property being rented' (Ribner, p. 110).
91 *fry*: offspring.
95 *vouchsafe*: please take.

CHARLEMONT. Guilty of killing him, but not of murder.
My lords, I have no purpose to desire
Remission for myself . . .

D'AMVILLE *descends to* CHARLEMONT.

D'AMVILLE. Uncivil boy! Thou want'st humanity to smile at grief. Why dost thou cast a cheerful eye upon the object of my sorrow, my dead sons?

1 JUDGE. O good my lord, let charity forbear
To vex the spirit of a dying man:
A cheerful eye upon the face of death
Is the true count'nance of a noble mind.
For honour's sake, my lord, molest it not.

D'AMVILLE. Y'are all uncivil. O, is't not enough that he unjustly hath conspired with Fate to cut off my posterity for him to be the heir to my possessions, but he must pursue me with his presence and in the ostentation of his joy laugh in my face and glory in my grief?

CHARLEMONT. D'Amville, to show thee with what light respect
I value death and thy insulting pride,
Thus, like a warlike navy on the sea,
Bound for the conquest of some wealthy land,
Passed through the stormy troubles of this life
And now arrived upon the armèd coast,
In expectation of the victory
Whose honour lies beyond this exigent,
Through mortal danger with an active spirit
Thus I aspire to undergo my death.

Leaps up the scaffold.

CASTABELLA *leaps after him.*

CASTABELLA. And thus I second thy brave enterprise.
Be cheerful, Charlemont: our lives cut off
In our young prime of years are like green herbs
Wherewith we strow the hearses of our friends;
For as their virtue, gathered when th'are green,
Before they wither or corrupt, is best;
So we in virtue are the best for death
While yet we have not lived to such an age
That the increasing canker of our sins

---

125 *exigent*: extremity.
136 *canker*: a sore which spreads unstoppably.

Hath spread too far upon us.
D'AMVILLE. A boon, my lords, I beg a boon.
1 JUDGE. What's that, my lord?
D'AMVILLE. His body, when 'tis dead, for an anatomy.
1 JUDGE. For what, my lord?
D'AMVILLE. Your understanding still comes short o'mine.
I would find out by his anatomy
What thing there is in nature more exact
Than in the constitution of myself.
Methinks my parts and my dimensions are
As many, as large, as well composed as his –
And yet in me the resolution wants
To die with that assurance as he does.
The cause of that, in his anatomy,
I would find out.
1 JUDGE. Be patient and you shall.
D'AMVILLE. I have bethought me of a better way.

Nephew, we must confer. Sir, I am grown a wondrous student now o'late. My wit has reached beyond the scope of nature, yet, for all my learning, I am still to seek from whence the peace of conscience should proceed.

CHARLEMONT. The peace of conscience rises in itself.

D'AMVILLE. Whether it be thy art or nature, I admire thee, Charlemont. Why, thou hast taught a woman to be valiant. I will beg thy life . . . My lords! I beg my nephew's life . . . I'll make thee my physician. Thou shalt read philosophy to me. I will find out th'efficient cause of a contented mind. But if I cannot profit in't then 'tis no more, being my physician, but infuse a little poison in a potion when thou giv'st me physic, unawares to me. So I shall steal into my grave without the understanding or the fear of death – and that's the end I aim at, for the thought of death is a most fearful torment is't not?

2 JUDGE. Your lordship interrupts the course of law.
1 JUDGE. Prepare to die.
CHARLEMONT. My resolution's made.
But ere I die, before this honoured bench,

---

140 *anatomy*: skeleton.
144 *exact*: perfect.
163 *efficient*: that which effects a certain end.

With the free voice of a departing soul
I here protest this gentlewoman clear
Of all offence the law condemns her for.

CASTABELLA. I have accused myself: the law wants power
To clear me. My dear Charlemont, with thee
I will partake of all thy punishments.

CHARLEMONT. Uncle, for all the wealthy benefits
My death advances you, grant me but this:
Your mediation for the guiltless life
Of Castabella, whom, your conscience knows
As justly clear as harmless innocence.

D'AMVILLE. Freely. My mediation for her life and all my int'rest in the world to boot, let her but in exchange possess me of the resolution that she dies withall. The price of things is best known in their want. Had I her courage, so I value it, the Indies should not buy't out o'my hands.

CHARLEMONT. Give me a glass of water.

D'AMVILLE. Me, of wine . . .
The argument of death congeals my blood;
Cold fear with apprehension of thy end
Hath frozen up the rivers of my veins . . .

A glass of wine.

I must drink wine to warm me and dissolve the obstruction or an apoplexy will possess me . . . Why, thou uncharitable knave, dost bring me blood to drink? The very glass looks pale and trembles at it.

SERVANT. 'Tis your hand, my lord.

D'AMVILLE. Canst blame me to be fearful, bearing still the presence of a murderer about me?

CHARLEMONT. Is this water?

SERVANT. Water, sir. *A glass of water.*

CHARLEMONT. Come thou clear emblem of cool temperance,
Be thou my witness that I use no art
To force my courage, nor have need of helps
To raise my spirits, like those weaker men
Who mix their blood with wine and out of that
Adulterate conjunction do beget
A bastard valour. Native courage, thanks.
Thou lead'st me soberly to undertake
This great, hard work of magnanimity.

D'AMVILLE. Brave Charlemont, at the reflexion of

thy courage my cold, fearful blood takes fire and I begin to emulate thy death . . . Is that thy executioner? My lords, you wrong the honour of so high a blood to let him suffer by so base a hand.

JUDGES. He suffers by the form of law, my lord.

D'AMVILLE. I will reform it. Down, you shag-haired cur. The instrument that strikes my nephew's head shall be as noble as his blood. I'll be thy executioner myself.

1 JUDGE. Restrain his fury. Good my lord, forbear.

D'AMVILLE. I'll butcher out the passage of his soul
That dares attempt to interrupt the blow.

2 JUDGE. My lord, the office will impress a mark
Of scandal and dishonour on your name.

CHARLEMONT. The office fits him, hinder not his hand,
But let him crown my resolution with
An unexampled dignity of death.
Strike home. Thus I submit me.

Ready for execution.

CASTABELLA. So do I:
In scorn of death thus hand in hand we die.

D'AMVILLE. I ha'the trick on't nephew. You shall see how eas'ly I can put you out of pain . . . Oh!

As he raises up the axe strikes out his own brains.
Staggers off the scaffold.

EXECUTIONER. In lifting up the axe I think h'as knocked his brains out.

D'AMVILLE. What murderer was he that lifted up my hand against my head?

1 JUDGE. None but yourself, my lord.

D'AMVILLE. I thought he was a murderer that did it.

2 JUDGE. God forbid.

D'AMVILLE. Forbid? You lie, judge. He commanded it, to tell thee that man's wisdom is a fool. I came to thee for judgement, and thou think'st thyself a wise man. I outreached thy wit and made thy justice murder's instrument in Castabella's death and Charlemont's, to crown my murder of Montferrers with a safe possession of his wealthy state . . .

---

217 *emulate*: imitate the manner of . . .
221 *shag-haired*: rough-haired.
229 *office*: i.e. of being executioner.
234 *ha'the trick*: have the knack.

CHARLEMONT. I claim the just advantage of his words.
1 JUDGE. Descend the scaffold and attend the rest.
D'AMVILLE. There was the strength of natural understanding. But nature is a fool: there is a power above her that hath overthrown the pride of all my projects and posterity, for whose surviving blood I had erected a proud monument, and struck 'em dead before me. For whose deaths I called to thee for judgement. Thou didst want discretion for the sentence, but yond' power that struck me knew the judgement I deserved and gave it . . . O, the lust of death commits a rape upon me as I would ha'done on Castabella . . .

Dies.

2 JUDGE. Strange is his death and judgement. With the hands
Of joy and justice I thus set you free.
The power of that eternal providence
Which overthrew his projects in their pride
Hath made your griefs th'instruments to raise
Your blessings to a greater height than ever.
CHARLEMONT. Only to heaven I attribute the work,
Whose gracious motives made me still forbear
To be mine own revenger. Now I see
That patience is the honest man's revenge.
1 JUDGE. Instead of Charlemont that but e'en now
Stood ready to be dispossessed of all,
I now salute you with more titles, both
Of wealth and dignity, than you were born to:
And you, sweet madam, lady of Belforest –
You have that title by your father's death.
CASTABELLA. With all the titles due to me increase
The wealth and honour of my Charlemont:
Lord of Montferrers, lord D'Amville, Belforest,
And for a close to make up all the rest,

They embrace.

The lord of Castabella. Now at last
Enjoy the full possession of my love,
As clear and pure as my first chastity.

251ff. See Textual note p. 197.
attend: listen to.
258 *discretion*: discernment.

CHARLEMONT. The crown of all my blessings! I will tempt
My stars no longer, nor protract my time
Of marriage. When those nuptial rites are done
I will perform my kinsmen's funerals.
2 JUDGE. The drums and trumpets! Interchange the sounds
Of death and triumph for those honoured lives
Succeeding their deservèd tragedies.
CHARLEMONT. Thus by the work of heav'n the men that thought
To follow our dead bodies without tears
Are dead themselves, and now we follow theirs.

Finis.

NOTES

TEXTUAL NOTES

The Revenger's Tragedy

I.i.2 *his*: her Q.

I.ii.42 *first*: so Q. Dodsley and some modern editors emend to 'fast', which is attractive but not strictly necessary since the Q. reading can have the sense of 'first offence'.

I.ii.65 *ceased*: several editors emend to 'cess'd' but the Q. reading makes sense – 'I could die more easily/naturally than through execution for this offence.'

I.ii.81 *Pox*: Pax Q.

I.ii.87–8 Prose in Q.

I.ii.135–9 Prose in Q.

I.ii.161 *commandément*: the stressed 'e' is necessary for the metre.

I.iii.17–18 Prose in Q.

I.iii.31–4 Prose in Q.

I.iii.183 *blood*: good Q., which is almost certainly a printer's drop from the line above.

I.iv.39 *heard*: hard Q.; the emendation is Dodsley's.

II.i.66 *in't*: it Q.; the emendation is Dodsley's.

II.i.84–5 Prose in Q.

II.i.90 *still fools*: still fool Q.

II.i.131 *madam*: Mad-man Q.; the emendation is Dodsley's.

II.i.149 *should*: shouldst Q.; the emendation is Dodsley's.

II.i.153 *others*: other Q.; the emendation is Dodsley's.

II.i.205–7 Prose in Q.

II.i.228 *love*: so Q.; Gibbons reads 'low', which fits well with 'dejected', but the Q. reading makes sense if 'love' is taken ironically.

II.ii.31–2 Prose in Q.

II.ii.55 *cheeks*: checkes Q.; the emendation is Dodsley's.

II.ii.148–50 I follow Nicoll and Gibbons in the disposition of these lines.

II.iii.15 *gripe*: so Q.; Gibbons emends to 'grip' but this seems unnecessary.

II.iii. 34 s.d. '*Exeunt . . . Hippolito*': Q. has s.d. 'dissemble at flight'.

II.iii.122 Gibbons omits 'Which' but the word is presumably meant as parallel to 'liberty' (l. 119).

III.i.15 *Blessed*: Blast Q.; the emendation is Dodsley's.

III.iii.14 *impúdent*: so Q.; some editors emend to 'imprudent' but Q. makes perfectly good sense.

III.iii.16 *sound*: so Q.; Gibbons reads 'found' but the phrase is echoed at III.iv.29 as 'sound' and the meaning is clear, anyway.

III.iv.22 So Q.: I see no reason to turn this into two non-decasyllabic lines as some editors do.

III.v,111 *fine*: Gibbons emends to 'sign', but Q.'s 'fine' (= a fine lady) is perfectly acceptable.

III.v.144–5 Prose in Q.

III.v.164 *slobbering*: flobbering Q.; the emendation is Hazlitt's – Q.'s reading is unfortunately not defensible.

IV.i.2 *Aught*: Ought Q.

IV.i. 74 s.d. '*The nobles enter*': Q. has these words in roman as part of Lussurioso's speech but they seem more likely to be a s.d.

IV.ii.65f. Q. gives this speech to Hippolito but it seems to fit better into the flow of conversation if given to Lussurioso, as Gilchrist suggests.

IV.ii.100 *pockets*: so Dodsley; Q. has 'pock', 'ets' having dropped to the line below.

IV.ii.218 *We*: Me Q.; Dodsley corrected the inverted letter.

IV.iv.14 *you powers*: so Q.; Swinburne conjectured the emendation 'Thou only God' and some editors follow this but there is little need.

IV.iv.132 *held*: Gibbons, following Collier, reads 'unfruitful child, tedious' but Q. is perfectly adequate.

IV.iv.157 *Buy*: so Q.; most editors emend to 'Be' (following Reed) and this is an attractive reading. Since, however, the Q. version makes sense I have retained it.

V.i.88 *Thus*: there is no need to emend to 'This' as Gibbons does.

V.i.90 *farthest*: fordest Q.; the emendation is Dodsley's.

V.i.96 Ross follows Dodsley in giving this line to Vindice, but I see no reason to depart from Q.'s version.

V.i.111 *I*: Gibbons reads 'Ay' for no reason I can follow.

V.i. 125 s.d. '*Exit . . . guarded*': Ross gives as s.d. 'Exeunt Gentlemen, guarded'. There is perhaps a slight muddle in the text here since the first gentleman is not singly culpable, but Lussurioso, at l. 122–3, has said 'Bear *him* straight To execution' and the picking on the spokesman seems typical both of Lussurioso and of the play's view of justice.

V.iii.53 Q. gives this line to Spurio but it clearly belongs to Supervacuo – the initial letter may have misled a tired or bored typesetter.

V.iii.60 *wake*: so Q.; Gibbons emends to 'make' and may well be right but Q. makes sense as it stands.

V.iii.88 *May*: Way Q.; Dodsley's inversion is necessary.

The Atheist's Tragedy

I.i.41 *industry*: industrie, Q.; industry, R.

I.ii.57 *commandéments*: so Q.; commandments, R. but the stressed 'e' is metrically necessary.

I.ii.63 *a-coming*: so R.; O'comming, Q.

I.ii.125–6 I follow the punctuation of Nicoll and Ribner here, to bring out the fact that 'joining' is in apposition to 'parting' (l. 124).

I.ii. 172 s.d. *Gives him a ring*: Gives him the ring, Q.

I.iv.47ff. I retain Q.'s prose for this speech rather than resetting as verse as most editors do. Languebeau usually uses prose and the lines gain little from resetting.

I.iv.106 *her good*: good, Q.: 'her' is Collins's sensible addition.

I.iv.129–31, 134–5 Q.'s prose is retained. Sebastian uses prose at l. 140ff. so it seems reasonable to retain it here.

II.i.28–44 I follow R. in resetting these lines (except those of the servant) as verse.

II.i. 111 s.d. In Q. the words 'The scarfe' appear in italics after a dash following 'life'. Some editors have taken the words as part of the speech, but they are clearly a stage direction.

II.ii.4 *t'wou't*: 'if thou wilt'. I follow Ribner's emendation of Q. t'wut.

II.iii.9–12 Ribner takes 'thou' as referring to heaven and, regarding 'Hadst . . . pleased' as a broken sentence, places a dash between 'pleased' and 'O'. I take 'Yet . . . pleased' as a complete sentence with the final clause referring back to 'Yet . . . enough'.

II.iv.7–23 Here again I retain Q.'s prose since little is gained by aligning it as verse as some editors do.

II.iv.31ff. This exchange between D'Amville and Belforest has been reset as verse because the emotional pitch seems to require it.

II.iv.141ff. D'Amville's speech has been realigned as verse.

II.v.13 *I*: Ribner's 'Ay' is surely wrong and Q.'s 'I', balancing Fresco's 'I' at l. 12, is clearly correct.

II.vi.s.d. Although the s.d. in Q. refers to the entry of a 'musquetier' the character is referred to as 'souldier' throughout the scene, so I have regularised this small inconsistency.

IV.iii.35 *costard-mongers*: Ribner follows Symonds in emending to 'costermongers', but the meaning is the same (a seller of fruit and vegetables).

IV.iii.65 *on*: an, Q.

IV.iii.198ff. I have retained Q.'s prose despite the importance of the speech because it loses force if set as verse (as verse the emphases are often clearly misleading or weak).

IV.iii.235–43 Q. gives this all to Languebeau but it seems clear that the passage from 'The ghost . . . ' should to go D'Amville, as is suggested by the comment of the watch at l. 244 – a remark which cannot be aimed at Languebeau.

V.ii.251ff. From this point on, Q. fails to distinguish between the two judges: I give them alternate speeches.

ADDITIONAL NOTES

The Revenger's Tragedy

V.iii.s.d. '*A blazing star*': Gibbons comments, 'a stage effect as simple, naive and half-comical as those in Miracle Plays' and goes on to mention Beckett as a modern parallel. How one 'reads' this piece of business must ultimately depend on one's overall view of the play; but I think Gibbons is misleading in using the words 'simple' and 'naive'. The Globe seems to have liked its blazing star and, of course, this type of divine portent was highly conventional by the time of this play. But this does not mean that the device was 'naive': in context of the play's metaphysical views it is complex and even profound as a symbol of the ambiguous nature of the universe as this dramatist sees it. What is perhaps more important is the suggested link with Beckett. The s.d. Gibbons quotes from *Waiting for Godot* has a kind of surreal effect which certainly includes the part-comic response of 'absurd' drama. I would agree with Gibbons that the blazing star in the context of *The Revenger's Tragedy* has something of the same effect, but the element of horror should not be understated – indeed the play is an extraordinary mixture of the comic and the appalling, and the total effect has quite a lot in common with black comedy.

V.iii.104 Gibbons comments, 'Thus Antonio provides an illustration of the general law propounded by Machiavelli: "He who is the cause of another becoming powerful is ruined; because that predominancy has been brought about either by astuteness or else by force, and both are distrusted by him who has been raised to power" ' (*The Prince*, trans. W.K. Marriott (London, 1908), ch. 3). It is highly important, for one's view of what sort of play *The Revenger's Tragedy* is, to decide how far the quotation from Machiavelli is apt, because if we accept its relevance we are involving Antonio in the game of power politics and intrigue which has made up the play's fabric. This, in turn, means that it is difficult to see Antonio as embodying any sense of tragic relief, of a world returning to normal. Instead we have the awful sense that what we have seen *is* the norm. I think myself that the quotation from Machiavelli is very important and I see the play as thoroughly pessimistic.

The Atheist's Tragedy

II.iv.146ff. This view of thunder has a classical background: Ribner (p. 46) cites Aristotle's *Meteorologia*, 363, and Lucretius's *De Rerum Natura*, but he also points out that there are contemporary accounts which Tourneur may have known of, and quotes from Digges:

> Thunder is the quenching of fyre, in a cloude. Or thunder is an exhalation, hot and dry, mixt with moisture caryed vp to the middle Region, there thicked and wrapped into a cloud, of this hot matter coupled in moystness, closed in the cloud, groweth a strife, the heate heatinge, and breaking out the sides of ye cloude with a thundringe noyse: the fyre then dispersed, is the lightninge.